# CLEM
## *The Story of a Raven*

*Jennifer Owings Dewey*

ILLUSTRATED BY THE AUTHOR

"On a cold, bright New Mexico morning, I awoke to a familiar sound, a hoarse croaking that broke the stillness of the early day. At once I knew what it was and who it was. It was Clem, the raven."

Jennifer Dewey tells the story of her family's relationship with a raven, blown from its nest as a baby and rescued by Keith, her husband. Here is a rare opportunity to enjoy the exciting experiences of Clem growing up— learning to fly, making caches throughout the house and yard of "found" objects, encountering neighboring farmyard animals, including piglets and chickens, rafting on the river. Join him when he first meets the somber Clyde, a burrowing owl that also shares their home, and baby Tamar, whom Clem fiercely protects.

This charming ...
with warmth a...
special view into ...

# CLEM
*The Story of a Raven*

# CLEM
## *The Story of a Raven*

WRITTEN AND ILLUSTRATED BY
## *Jennifer Owings Dewey*

DODD, MEAD & COMPANY     NEW YORK

1   2   3   4   5   6   7   8   9   10

Library of Congress Cataloging-in-Publication Data

Dewey, Jennifer.
    Clem: the story of a raven.

    Summary: The author describes her family's experiences raising
and caring for a raven from babyhood to adulthood when he returns
to the wild.
    1. Ravens—Juvenile literature.  [1. Ravens]  I. Title.
QL795.B57D49  1986      636.6        85-27440
ISBN 0-396-08728-0

*For Tamar, Keith, and Clem*

# CONTENTS

# Late Spring

On a cold, bright New Mexico morning I awoke to a familiar sound, a hoarse croaking that broke the stillness of the early day. At once I knew what it was and who it was. It was Clem, the raven.

Only a few weeks earlier Clem had flown off for what I supposed would be the last time. He had been leaving in the afternoons and staying away all night more and more frequently. Then for several days he did not return at all. Now here he was. Back again.

I went outside and looked up. The air was clear. High overhead a dark shape traced wide circles

9

in the sky. I shaded my eyes with my hand and watched Clem's wings rise and fall. His powerful head hung down a little, and his huge beak was slightly open.

His wings carried him up and around, then into a long, smooth glide toward the ground.

Ravens build nests in trees, on cliffs, or sometimes in abandoned buildings, using hundreds of sticks. In places where sticks are hard to find, they use the bones of dead animals, or even baling or barbed wire. Fur, deer hair, moss, grass—any soft debris—becomes their nest lining.

Clem's mother had built her nest near the top of a pine tree, where it had little shelter from gusting winds. Late in the spring a fierce storm had ripped the nest apart, plunging four nestlings to the forest floor. A hiker discovers the accident a few hours later. Near the base of the tree, on the ground, lay three lifeless baby ravens. A fourth sat shivering, almost out of sight under a bush. The hiker brings the fourth baby raven home in the bowl of his hat. The hiker is my husband, Keith.

Ravens are big birds. Full grown, they stand as tall as a large house cat and weigh about two pounds. I have never seen a baby raven before. This baby is a damp, almost featherless handful, stunned and miserable, weighing less than a pound. Its wrinkled, raw-looking skin is dotted with patchy tufts of down and a few twisted, rumpled feathers. About six inches long, as wide as my hand when I make a fist, its bony body looks like it would fall apart if its skin didn't hold it together.

Keith and I know enough about birds to recognize this wet baby as a raven. But we need to know more. We look ravens up in the bird guide: Common Raven, member of the crow family, subfamily Corvinae. Other relatives are rooks, nutcrackers, jackdaws, and crows. From the down on its upper body, and the few crumpled feathers growing at odd angles out of its wings, we judge it to be about two weeks old.

We name the baby Clem almost immediately. We like the sound of the name and it is easy to say. When we name him we agree it will be all right if he turns out to be "Clementine."

Clem is all head, stomach, and enormous beak. His body looks too large for his skinny legs. He cannot stand up, and fluttering his wings makes his head wobble. A thin bluish membrane half closes over his eyes every now and then. (This membrane is called the "third eyelid" in adult birds, and protects the eyes in flight.) When I hold Clem cupped in my hands I feel the rhythm of his heart beating against his chest.

His beak is a translucent whitish-gray, like wax

paper. Inside his beak, along the upper edge, the bluish-gray turns to bright yellow. A thick red tongue shaped like a cone moves forward and back when Clem's beak is open. (As a brand-new baby, Clem's beak is open most of the time.) Looking down his throat I feel I can see all the way to his stomach.

Right from the start we love this big, ugly baby. And right from the start he loves us back.

After drying Clem off we line a cardboard box with a soft, woolly scarf and pieces of old towels. Clem appears to accept this substitute nest. Perhaps the high sheltering sides of the box remind him of his original home.

Resting gently on the bottom, Clem relaxes. His eyelids close over his eyes, his head drops on his chest, and he sleeps. We begin to think about what to feed him.

We know wild ravens eat almost anything, so we decide to offer Clem a variety of foods to take the place of the insects, worms, and carrion his real mother would give him. There is no need to be delicate about feeding this baby bird, no need for eyedroppers or other special devices to coax food down his throat.

After twenty or thirty minutes of sleep Clem awakens and he squawks vigorously, his beak open as far as it will go, his eyes imploring: FEED ME! We do—bread soaked in milk, dog food softened in warm water, crumbled hard-boiled eggs. He loves milk-toast with honey, Mandarin orange segments, and pinto beans. Whatever the food, we simply hold it over Clem's open beak and drop it in, three to twelve meals a day, round the clock.

He seems not to swallow. The food disappears into his enormous maw and reappears almost immediately at the tail end. We can watch its progress,

13

since there are so few feathers covering his skin. The lumps pass through at breakneck speed. Is it our imagination or does he eject more than he takes in? This is impossible. Somehow he gains nourishment, despite his rapid-fire digestive system. Hunger calls, loud, long and pitiful, turn to low, soft gurgles once Clem's stomach is "filled."

For the first three days Clem does little but sleep and eat, eat and sleep. He sleeps for three or four hours and then is ready to be fed again. This goes on morning and night. His sounds tell us what state he is in: hungry, satisfied, or somewhere between one and the other.

Clem's Latin name is *Corvus corax*. We read that *corax* comes from the Greek word *korax*, meaning "a croaker." A fitting name for this baby raven. He can make soft, gentle sounds or ear-piercing screeches. His sounds are not birdsong—raven sounds are more language than song.

Wild ravens communicate with a wide repertoire of croaks, gurgles, growls, coos, caws, screeches, screams, cackles, and rattles. There are alarm calls, assembly calls, mating, and scolding calls. Flocks have identifying calls, and so do individuals. Bursts of caws, usually six or seven to a burst, short or long, with varying pauses between, establish identifying patterns. Messages are being passed.

Clem communicates to us with coos and grunts—

rumbles of sounds that seem to come from his belly, not his vocal chords. Within a few days of his arrival we recognize patterns and repetitions. His urgent "CAWCAWCAW!!" announces he is hungry. His "CROAKCROAKCROAK" tells us he is happy for the moment. A series of soft gurgles tells us he is drifting off to sleep.

We wonder: what does a baby raven want? What does it need? We wonder what a real mother raven and nestlings provide that we have no hope of providing. We decide, without thinking about it consciously, to raise him. He would not survive in the wild. There are too many dogs, cats, and other dangers for one so defenseless as Clem. We talk about how to keep such an unusual pet. We agree it will be best to keep him free. We will not clip his wings, nor keep him caged. We will allow him access to the real world.

The first ten days Clem spends in or near his box. He is content to be lifted out by hand and placed gently on the floor. Much of the time he is groggy, even stupid. His insatiable appetite rules him. Empty, he screeches for food; full, he sleeps a deep and satisfied sleep. We watch him—and with gleaming blue-black eyes he watches us. We listen to his wet, gurgling croaks, and we wonder; does he dream? Do baby birds have thoughts? How difficult it is not to assume things about him.

On a diet of all sorts of unbirdfood-like things, Clem grows. We feed him bananas, vanilla pudding, applesauce, and strawberries. Keith holds Clem on his knee, securing him with one large hand. Bulky and black, feathered like a pincushion, Clem tips his head back, opens his beak, and Keith drops bits of ripe, mashed banana down his throat. Clem accepts the firm grip of Keith's hand.

Clumps of grayish-brown down fall out, and feathers grow in on Clem's wings, chest, and sides. At first his feathers appear in rows, like stripes on a uniform. In between the rows is wrinkled, naked skin. Tailfeathers also grow. These are half as long as his adult tailfeathers will be, but they help him keep his balance when he hops across the floor, which he tries to do within five days of his arrival. He flutters his wings, loses his balance, tries again. Finally he hops without falling over. These first journeys never take him far—and he almost always has to be carried back to his box.

Clem is curious. Like a pond beetle sensitive to surface changes in light and motion, once out of his box he becomes increasingly alert to anything new in the room. If it is something small, he notices it. If it is something big, he reacts. A tiny bug blown in on the breeze, a human visitor, a moth fluttering in a corner—Clem wants to investigate.

Unsteady on his legs, a drunken sailor of a bird

16

weaving his way from one place to another, Clem begins to explore his world.

The sun is low, near setting. A fretful breeze stirs in the yard. The window is up a little, a small space open to the world—enough to allow explosions of dust to burst in every now and then. Beams of dusty light penetrate the glass.

I have lifted Clem out of his box, and he waddles across the floor. He resembles an old man on unreliable legs. The center of gravity is off—equilibrium is questionable. He swerves to avoid a chair leg, loses his balance, regains it, loses it again. A tumble seems inevitable but does not come.

Sunlight splashes on the floor and Clem stands in it. He blinks, cocks his head, twists it around so that one eye is concentrated on the opening where

the puffs of dust blow in. He makes a grumbling noise in his throat. Weak, scantily feathered wings beat up and down.

His awkwardness immobilizes him. He squats down on the floor, curiosity fixing him to his spot of light.

The sun sets. The wind dies. The light is gone. Clem sits, forlorn and alone, a rumpled lump on the floor. He croaks for someone to come and rescue him. He does not have the energy to make it back to his box.

Before long his cry is a fierce command—a shrill "SQUAWKSQUAWK!" that brings me running. Gently lifting him in two hands I feel, as well as see, his distress. His body quakes, just as a baby trembles when it has cried too long. His eyes are half-closed. It does not take much adventure to consume his energy.

We have another bird in the house. My husband, a teacher of sculpture, has been given a "homeless" burrowing owl by one of his students. The owl was pathetic when he arrived: not a nestling like Clem, but a half-grown, poorly fed, mite-infested little waif with staring eyes and no sense of humor. We named him Clyde. Somehow he looked like a Clyde, though most of the time he was called Owl.

Owl's legs are long and skinny, his body hardly more than a handful of feathers with a proud thrust behind them. His eyes are as yellow as sunflowers, with black irises that grow and shrink in accordance with the brightness of the light. His beak is small, tan in color, yellow on the inside edge, and sharply hooked. He uses it to shred wings from beetles, pierce sinewy chicken gizzards, and cut crackly grasshoppers into "bite-sized" pieces. Bristles and feathers around his beak conceal his mouth, which is surprisingly large and has ridges on its inside surface. When Owl closes his eyes he appears to have no eyes at all. With eyelids down, the pattern of the feathers on his face is all of a piece.

Owl usually stands on a perch Keith made for him—a platform secured to the top of a pole. People come and go. Sometimes they ask: "What does he *DO* all day?" We say: "He stands there and looks around. He takes baths. He eats." His place on his perch is his dry ground, his sanctuary.

Clyde is not remarkable unless his self-possession can be called remarkable. He has more of that than any bird, or any creature, I have ever known. As a newcomer he did not take to us. He had already learned something, but we did not know just what.

Clyde is often free to roam about the house. He is rarely outside because he is not a good flyer

and would be an easy mark for any dog or cat with predatory intentions. And he might run away. We are not sure that he won't.

In his best moods Owl likes to perch on Keith's shoulder, or knee, and look around. But he has his other moods—times when he hides in a corner for hours, or refuses to leave his perch.

A burrowing owl's flight is almost silent. There is the slightest murmur of feathers, the hint of rushing air. One moment Clyde is on his perch, the next he stands regally on the edge of Clem's box, about to lose his balance but refusing to admit it. He glares into the box, his gaze fixed on the dark form curled into the rags and woolly scarf at the bottom. Clyde does not communicate with sound. But he observes, and we can tell he senses there is something new in the house, and that that something is a bird.

In the wild, burrowing owls would have little to do with ravens. Nor would ravens find burrowing owls, scampering around on the ground, especially interesting. At this first meeting between Clyde and Clem nothing much happens. Gripping the top edge of Clem's box with his sharp talons, Clyde cautiously circumnavigates it. Clem looks up and blinks. Too young, too fuzzy-headed to take in the feathery object perched above him, he nods his heavy head a few times and goes back to sleep. Clyde flies from Clem's box to a corner of the room and starts grooming his feathers, chittering softly to himself.

At first, Clem does not seem to notice Clyde much. And I wonder, in those early days, if Owl does not try rather hard to ignore Clem. Once I catch Clyde staring at Clem. He hangs by his claws from the pull cord of a screen, half upside-down, watching for a long time. Clem is sitting in a spot of sunlight on the floor. Clyde seems to be forming opinions behind his bright yellow eyes.

Clyde likes spots of sunlight, too. Spreading himself on the floor, wings and tail fanned out, stretched as far as he can go, letting the sunlight penetrate his feathers. But he never has much time for leisure. Tightly strung, like a violin wire, Clyde is tense and watchful. The slightest noise sends him off to a corner or back to his perch.

Mountains stand to the east of us. Rising to nine thousand feet, they are blue in the distance. We go there often to hike and explore. Keith found Clem in these mountains.

To the west is a valley with a river running through it. The low places along the river are thick with cottonwood trees, willow, and tamarisk. Russian olives grow there, too, their pale silvery-green color offset by the red of the tamarisk branches and the gray-green of the willows. It is a woodsy place where we love to walk.

Our house lies two miles east of the river. Alfalfa and corn grow in the fields toward the river, and in the field behind us there is an apple orchard. It is very old, with gnarled, overgrown trees, stumps half-covered with vines, thistles, and dandelions.

We live by a dirt road that runs from the town, ten miles away, into the countryside. We have neighbors to the north and to the south.

Our house is really an old ruin that Keith and I are restoring to something livable. It is an adobe house, built of mud-and-straw bricks. All around the yard piles of bricks, trowels, hoes, a wheelbarrow, sand and gravel and earth for plastering walls, shovels and pails, hammers and boxes of nails, all bespeak the fact that labors on the house dominate daily life. Whole walls have yet to be built when Clem arrives late in the spring.

Keith's blue eyes squint against the sun's glare while he unloads adobes off the delivery truck. He is tall and blond with strong arms and hands. He lets his beard grow in the spring and summer. Wisps of his hair blow in the breeze. This is our first house together, and our first experience building with adobe bricks. We have finished only one room, the room we live in. And we all live in it: Owl, raven, husband and wife.

23

A lot of work remains to be done when we hang the cradle from the ceiling for our baby, a girl we name Tamar, who arrives when Clem is one month old.

# First Summer

In the hanging cradle the baby sleeps, making small, dreamy sounds. Owl stands stiff-legged on his platform, one foot resting on the remnant of a chicken neck. Clem is under the cradle on the floor, legs set wide apart, head bent back, staring up. Owl is aloof; Clem is curious. I lift Clem up and hold him close to the sleeping baby. He seems not to pay attention, but nevertheless I think he takes her in.

Morning. Magpies and mockingbirds calling outside, and inside Clem's madcap antics. Hoots and cackles announce he is wide awake and ready

25

for another day. He knows no melody, offers no harmony, but his enthusiasm is infectious. All in the room are cheered to hear him—all but Clyde, who fixes Clem's box with a malignant glare. Clem's vocal displays interrupt Clyde's morning peace.

At a month and a half, Clem is a bigger bird. He walks without his former inebriated lope. He still wobbles and rolls, like a ball floating on water, but he can manage a quick series of hops if he chooses to.

Each foot has four long, scaly toes with grayish-black, very sharp toenails. His big strong beak is better supported by his neck, and a sharp hook is forming at its end. He can pull and tug at things and not lose his balance. Bristly feathers now grow around his nostrils, and the feathers on his wings overlap each other, providing better coverage. He still has patches of skin where there are no feathers, but they are confined to his underbelly and the area under his wings. All the tufts and puffs of down are gone. His wings are stronger now and clearly help him keep his balance when he hops.

Clem now feeds himself. A dish of something—cooked hamburger or dog food—placed next to him on the floor is noisily and rapidly consumed. He draws the lower half of his beak across the dish, scraper-fashion, taking up chunks of food as he goes. Once the food is inside his beak his head tips back and the food can be seen traveling down his throat in lumps. Again his head dives down to the dish, his beak open about a third of the way, the lower half scooping. Clem also eats "found" objects—a lazy beetle crawling across the floor, a nocturnal moth sleeping in a corner. He likes raw food once in a while—morsels of gizzard or liver from a chicken I am fixing, or bits of fresh trout.

We feed Clem ourselves—getting down on hands and knees and offering him some delicacy from our own plates. Keith gives Clem scrambled eggs, bacon, and sliced tomatoes. Clem likes the attention and he likes the food. He never turns anything down.

Owl will not eat tomatoes, cheese, or toast. Owl will eat only meat, or insects and mice he finds on his tours around the inside of the house. He eats grasshoppers, crickets, spiders, and moths. He eats meat from the store: raw steak, or chicken necks, hearts, and gizzards. We never hand-feed Owl. For him, eating is a private matter—a secretive thing. We put chunks of meat on his platform and turn away, not wishing to invade his privacy.

There are skills, bird-skills, Clem has to learn. Keith and I realize that birds in the wild have to learn certain skills, but it is a revelation to us that Clem has to practice standing on one leg.

Many birds are able to rest on one leg. Drawing the other leg up under the body, tucking the head under a neck ruff or breast feathers, a bird stands watchful and aware, yet resting. Clem tries: he pulls one leg up—it bends in and out erratically. The supporting leg gives a little—not a good sign. The

lifted leg goes down, or else Clem teeters over, using his wings to save himself, swinging his head in circles as if this might help. It is impossible to say when everything finally comes together. One day

29

Clem is still trying. The next he is up on one leg, looking steady.

Clem's domain is the floor. He flops down, legs bent under him, sitting and blinking half-comprehending blinks at the world around him. Owl swoops past or scurries by. Owl often scurries, on errands only Owl knows about. Sitting on a stool at his workbench Keith is examining the multifarious inside parts of a nonfunctioning electric drill. All the pieces of the drill, both large and small, are spread out before him. Tamar is sleeping in her hanging cradle. Keith made the cradle for her—out of flat, smooth strips of steel welded together into the shape of half a clam shell. It is lined with a soft pad. A rope laced around the side keeps the cradle stabilized and supports it as it hangs.

Clem is underfoot a lot. He often falls asleep wherever he happens to be. If he is in shadow he is hard to see and almost gets stepped on. The brick floor has cracks and Clem likes to poke his beak into them. He dislodges tiny bugs or wads of dust. He hides under our bed, pulls at the bedcovers that hang down, unknowingly dumping things on top of himself, and falls asleep inside Keith's sneaker.

Keith's workbench is a complicated place. Boxes of tools, scraps of sculpture materials, extension cords, files filled with papers (the kind we can never throw away), and other things we don't need right now—all are kept in quiet disarray under the workbench. Clem squeezes himself between the boxes, crawls over the bags and files, disappears for half an hour at a time under and behind Keith's things. When he comes out he usually has spider webs draped over his head and around his eyes: a strange bride with a veil of dusty spider silk.

When Clem is nearly two months old he leaves his nestbox forever. We set up a roosting place for him: a chicken-wire enclosure, three feet across and two feet high, level with the floor and open on one side, with a stick stuck through to serve as a perch.

It is a hot day. Sitting with Tamar naked on my knees I watch Clem climb onto his new perch

for the very first time. He grabs the chicken-wire with his beak and tries to swing his body up to reach the stick and stand on it. He misses. He lets go of the chicken-wire and stands, still looking— staring—as if pondering what to do next. He tries the same maneuver a second time, and it works. The entire structure quivers from his weight, and I see it will have to be nailed down, but Clem is, in the end, triumphant on his own perch.

A dust storm has left a fine, grayish-brown powder everywhere: on windowsills, doorsills—any place there is a crack to let air in. Clem leaves tracks wherever he goes. He ambles along on the windowsills leaving delicate lines, the imprints of his toes. He bends his head down to slide his beak across the film of dust, and he breathes particles into his nostrils. It makes him pant.

Clem is constantly on the move, an intrepid hunter after spiders and flies. He gets stuck between bookcases, explores the shadowy damp world under the kitchen sink, and takes naps in corners laced with dust.

At two months he is impossible to keep indoors. It is time to introduce him to the front yard. One morning we carry him out and set him down by the front door. Keith holds Tamar under her arms, leaving her feet to dangle and "dance" in the air.

Together the three of us sit and watch the raven.

At first he seems surprised. This is a much bigger world, no longer the four familiar walls, a room full of well-known objects. Everything has been replaced by entirely new elements: brighter light, trees and bushes, gravel under his toes.

Clem stands still and looks around. His dark eyes glow. Before long he is hopping off. He raises his wings and flaps them, but without lowering them very far. This action gives him some "lift"—and increases the speed of his hops. He almost leaps into the air. Running along, wings up, head lowered, he looks like Groucho Marx in a cape. Along the ditchbank he becomes lost in shadows, then emerges where sunlight and shadow meet. He plunges into a pile of rotting leaves, climbs to the top of a mound of grass cuttings, and discovers something crawling along the ground under his feet.

Ants—red ants. Clem's first look at ants. He is standing on top of an anthill. The ants are frantic. The precise order of their colony has been disrupted

33

by this bird's big feet. They race in every direction. Using his beak, Clem flicks ants off the ground and into the air. He watches them fall. With his tongue thrust forward he draws an ant into his mouth. Instant reaction: his tongue moves in and out rapidly, his head bobs, he shakes his head, he scrapes his beak across the ground. He starts hopping in a tight little circle. When I check his mouth I see he has been bitten. A large red welt has risen on the side of his tongue. It is nothing serious—but Clem never again plays games with this army.

Beetles, crickets, drowsy flies, and moths, all are toys for an energetic raven. Once in a while he shows an interest in eating them. Usually he just enjoys them. When his games look too much like torture, I intervene. He might not want to be diverted from what he is doing—but he quickly finds something else to do.

On this first time outside Clem makes some important discoveries. There is a stinkbug lumbering across the yard. Clem does a dance around it. The bug assumes stinkbug threat posture: head down, tail in the air. Clem lowers his head and takes the bug into his beak. For a brief moment the bug is poised there, legs flying wildly. Then Clem drops it. He is off, once more shaking his head and bobbing around. The bug continues its trek across the yard, its "stink" having had the desired effect.

Later, Clem learns to eat stinkbugs in a special way. He knows that stinkbugs emit a vile-smelling secretion from their tail ends when they stand on their heads. So he grabs a stinkbug in his beak, rams it tail-first into the ground, and proceeds to eat it, starting with the head. The bug is not able to release its dose of stink with its tail pressed firmly against hard ground. Clem always eats the whole bug.

On this, his first day out, Clem discovers a fat, sleepy toad, under an old piece of wood. Expecting the animal to crawl away, or stand up, or in some way react, Clem is visibly frustrated when the toad does nothing. Clem persists. He jabs and nudges it with his beak. The toad remains inert, slumberous from heat and contentment. Clem's attentions begin to wane. Something tells him the green bump is alive, but it won't respond. About the time Clem loses interest, the toad makes a great leap into the air and hops off into the bushes. Too surprised to follow, Clem stays where he is and tosses the leaf litter, once the toad's bed, into the air. The stuff comes down around his head, a rainshower of wet decay. Remnants of leaf clinging to the feathers on top of his head, he wobbles off to his next adventure.

A big cottonwood tree stands by the front door. The tree is a gathering place, winter and summer, for all manner of birds. Magpies bounce from limb to limb and set the leaves to fluttering and rustling. Robins, meadowlarks, sparrows, and crows all visit the tree. The high sharp sounds of small birds mix with the low, grumbly sounds of larger birds as all sit and groom their feathers. Clem's presence outdoors has the effect of attracting certain birds: Jays, ravens, crows, and magpies visit more frequently and come in greater numbers. A pair of magpies visits the tree frequently, perching on a favorite branch, just out of reach over our heads.

Magpies are animated corvids, smaller than ravens and members of the subfamily Garrulinae. Striking black-and-white feathers and long black-and-white tails flash like light when they fly. Their songs bubble, whistle, and click as they mimic what they hear around them. Magpie pairs mate for life.

A young raven exploring weeds, tossing up rotting leaves, or scratching in the gravel inspires the magpie pair to be bold. Together they fly off their branch, land on the ground, and begin to hop up and down. The young raven reacts with obvious glee: two loud and aggressive playmates to romp with. And romp they do. Bird-babble fills the air: cawing and screeching from the magpies, a croaking rattle from Clem. The magpies never come too close; they are quick to bounce away as if they know the limits of their welcome. The games are quick to

36

begin and quick to end. The two magpies, acting
as a pair, bound up to Clem, face him boldly and
screech loudly, then bow low before turning around
and flying off. They repeat this, over and over:
moving up close to Clem, then bowing and turning
and flying away. One minute the three birds circle
each other on the ground, their movement sending
up sprays of pebbles. The next the magpies streak
off into the cottonwoods, their sounds lingering long
after their forms are lost to view.

It is good for Clyde to be out in the sunshine once in a while, and we put him on his outdoor perch by the front door when we know we will be close by to watch him. He is secured to his perch by jesses—leather straps attached to a tiny ring around one of his ankles. He scratches around on his platform, blinking, glaring, staring at the world through eyelids at half-mast.

If the magpie pair come by, they take great joy in dive-bombing Clyde. They zoom down on him from their branch, cawing and screaming, until Clyde flattens himself so firmly against his perch he virtually disappears. He is still there, of course, but his effort to make himself invisible is amazingly

39

successful. The harassment does not go on for long because we take him indoors—to his inside perch—where he can resume his posture of self-possession. The only time he is peaceful on his outside perch is when the magpies do not come. He is left in peace often enough for Keith and me to continue to take him outside. Sunshine is essential for Clyde's well-being.

Rubbing Clyde's bony chest with the knuckle of one finger, I think about what a dull life he leads. Fragile, stoic little Owl: one day is so like another for you!

Every day we work outside on our house, laying up new walls of adobe brick. A wooden trough about six feet long and a foot deep holds a mixture of sand, dirt, water, and straw that will become the mud used to hold the bricks together. Each brick weighs about twenty-four pounds. A layer of mud goes down, then a layer of bricks, then another layer of mud. Spaces are left for windows and doorways, corners are rounded and sculpted to make sure rainwater runs off properly. It is hard, satisfying work.

Airborne insects humming, the slap-slap-slap of mud being spread, once in a while a car out on the road—these are the only sounds. Tamar sleeps in her basket set out under a tree. Drops of perspiration roll down my neck as I hand Keith an adobe brick every time he's ready for one. We work in silence. We both notice Clem—walking by us covered with mud. He has mud on his lower body and all down his legs. He staggers a little from the unfamiliar weight. How did he get like this?

Keith sits on the ground to rest and I sit next to him. Together we watch Clem climb into the trough of mud and with "swimming" motions crawl through the sticky, wet stuff like a ship moving through thick ice. When he gets to the top end of the trough he climbs out—laboriously because of all the mud. He does this several times. Keith turns on the hose and makes a gentle spray of the water flow. He sprinkles water at Clem. Clem likes it. He stands still, his legs far apart, his head back and his beak half-open, allowing the water to flow down over him: a cool wash down on a hot afternoon.

Often Clem sits and observes our work, but usually he struts around and gets into things. I keep an eye on him just as I keep an eye on Tamar. Tamar is outside with us when we are out. And when we are inside she is with us, usually sleeping in her cradle hung from the ceiling.

Sitting on an old stump in the orchard to nurse Tamar becomes a daily habit. The apple trees are coming back to life. They have been ignored for years, but we water them and the soil around them

41

begins to be thick with grasses and weeds. Years before the ground had been plowed. Furrows remain, reaching up to where the next field begins. Now dandelions grow in the furrows, and Clem hops up and down getting dandelion fluff on his feathers. He turns up a wealth of bug life around the wet bases of the apple trees.

He finds a tomato hornworm. It is bright green, fat and bulbous, with parasitic wasp eggs attached to its back. The wasp larvae will feed off the worm while they develop and grow. In the end it will be the life of the wasps over the life of the worm.

Clem carries his prize around for a long time—for twenty minutes or more—swinging it back and forth under his bill like a thick piece of string. He does not kill it. He seems to like the way it swings to and fro. Eventually he drops it. I am glad he does not eat it.

Clem is protective of Tamar. While we work outdoors we drape a piece of cheesecloth over her basket to keep bugs away. Clem pulls it off and sits perched on the side of the basket, on guard duty, his big black feet gripping the basket edge, his body tipping this way and that as he tries to maintain his balance. He turns his head from side to side and bobs it up and down, fixing one or the other eye on whatever object he wishes to see. This turning

and cocking of his head seems to help him focus.
Intruders are announced with a warning call.

If Tamar is indoors in her cradle, Clem often
sits under it. If Tamar cries, he paces in circles,
around and around—especially when her crying

43

goes on for some time. When she quiets down, Clem stops pacing. During night feedings Clem often wakes up and joins Tamar and me. Waddling over to where I sit, nudging my leg with his beak, he makes known his presence. He loves to sit on my shoulder while I nurse Tamar. I lift him up in my hands and tuck him against my neck. He nestles down and stays still while I feed the baby. Sometimes all three of us fall asleep briefly. When I lay Tamar back into her bed, I put Clem down on the floor and he returns to his perch.

Hot July noontimes. Owl is usually inside on these hot days. (He would be in his burrow in the ground if he were wild and free.) Clem stands on the top of a wooden table with benches, under the cottonwood tree. Lunch is laid out. In my arms Tamar nurses. Clem steps closer for a look. With a jerky walk, his tail raised and twitching, he twists his head around to gaze at her out of one eye. The baby concerns him. Perhaps she takes the place of his lost nestmates? He stands there, very still, until he is certain all is well. If Tamar happens to be fussing or crying, Clem becomes agitated. He jumps from table to bench, from bench to ground, from ground back to table—around and around in irregular circles—jittery and disquieted, in motion until Tamar settles down. Then his attention is directed to his next meal.

**44**

Clem bounces around on the tabletop squawking for a handout. We cooperate with him. He makes a game of it by bobbing, bowing, turning in circles, turning his head half upside-down, and generally acting the clown in between each bite.

Our food is simple—and cold. The days are too hot for cooking. We eat oranges and pears, melons and strawberries. Clem eats everything we eat.

One day Clem discovers chocolate ice cream. I drop a little down his open mouth one noon. I do not think much about it until a minute later I feel him tugging at my shirt and poking me, making sibilant sounds in his chest. The sound is his "Feed me" sound. I realize he is serious. I give him another bite. Again he pokes me. His persistence finally wins. I put my dish down and let him have it. He eats all my ice cream. He loves it. After that Clem always has to have his own dish. His dish is just like Keith's and mine, the same size, the same flavor. Clem becomes addicted to a daily portion of chocolate ice cream. There is a crisis in the house if I discover we have run out.

Watching Clem eat ice cream shows me how his tongue and beak coordinate. His large thick tongue fills up the lower half of his beak when he lifts and thrusts it forward. He moves his tongue up and down, and flicks it forward and back, to draw food down his throat. He uses it in a similar way when drinking. His tongue "at rest" lies pulled back and tucked down into the lower half of his beak, seeming much smaller than it really is.

Ice cream is Clem's favorite, but he also loves corn on the cob (even after the kernels have been gnawed off), tomatoes, and popcorn. He eats numerous raisins, grapes, and peeled cucumbers. (He doesn't like cucumber skin.) He eats hamburgers—we give him everything at least once—by shredding and tearing, with beak and talons, until he has a pile of bite-sized pieces. He mangles and eats fruitcake the same way. He loves sugar cubes but he doesn't get many because we agree they might be bad for him.

Owl indulges in rituals when he eats: A mouse is always beheaded before being eaten. A cricket or a beetle is likewise dispatched before going down. For Clem it is never this way. Clem gorges, he experiments, he exhibits unlimited enthusiasm and no shame. The worst is when he pulls a centipede off the wall (a very large one) and eats it. I know it is his business, his stomach. I have no right to project my horror onto him. But I do. As he breaks the centipede into even pieces and swallows it, I have to turn away. I should be grateful to Clem for lowering the population of spiders and centipedes

46

in our house (it is high) but I am not. It is more fun to watch him eat chocolate ice cream.

Clem uses his large, strong beak as a poker, a probe, a scraper, and a hammer. As he grows, the bowed shape of his beak becomes more pronounced. He is deft and quick with it—flipping beetles upside-down, cleaning his plate of the last crumb of food, opening latches, banging on the doorframe when he wants out.

Knowing Clem uses his beak to probe and explore, I experience some alarm when I watch him lower his head to within inches of Tamar's face. Tamar is attracted by the bird's motions. She lies on her back and waves her arms while Clem, perched on the edge of her basket, bends as close to her as he can without actually touching her. I learn not to

47

worry. Somehow Clem knows: babies are to be watched, not poked.

Clem learns to use his beak to unlatch screen doors, open the mailbox, and get into and out of the bathroom cabinet. He takes nails, screws, paintbrushes, lids to things, pieces of mail, and baby socks. The laundry hamper is one of his favorite places. Sometimes I find him wandering across the yard dragging a piece of clothing in his beak. He seems to appreciate detail: The more objects he finds gathered in one place the happier he is.

He can jump, leap, and hold on tight with his big black feet. One day he attaches himself to the screen door, about halfway up the screen, and uses his beak to unhitch the latch. Cabinet doors are no trouble at all: Inserting his beak into the doorpull, he tugs at it until it opens. He loves to go into the cabinet under the bathroom sink. Here he explores—and with his beak and feet tosses most of the contents onto the floor. Keith's toolboxes, his boxes of many tiny screws and nails, are pure heaven to Clem. Everything of this kind has to be kept shut, even locked, if we are to be absolutely certain Clem will not invade and make off with things. Organic, inorganic, shiny or dull, he spurns nothing he can grasp and carry. One day Clem takes one of my paintbrushes. He takes diaper pins, the caps to oil-paint tubes, tubes themselves (the empties).

Wild ravens, jays, and other members of the corvid family commonly cache, or store, food. In the wild, caching frees extra time in the spring for nest building and caring for the young. Caching helps birds survive long, cold winters. Some corvids have special pouches for storing food. Ravens swallow food and regurgitate it at the cache. Clem regurgitates food, too, and sometimes we find one of his caches by following an evil smell.

Clem's collections: under the bathroom sink, behind the cedar chest, under the workbench, in depressions in the ground—often at the bases of trees.

One such depression, at the base of the cottonwood tree, holds several small stones. I decide to put the stones into a low-sided open box and leave the box on the ground near the place the stones had been. On impulse I add three stones to the box.

A few days later I notice that the "extra" stones

49

are missing. This time I decide to take some away. I take three.

Later I look and find three more stones have been put into the box—to replace the three I had taken. At first I do not believe Clem capable of "counting." I experiment a few more times, taking and leaving stones. I start making rows of stones: a row of three, a row of five, a row of four.

Clem nearly always replaces, or removes, the "correct" number of stones. He keeps the rows in order.

I start leaving other objects, things like rubber bands, toothpaste tubes (empty ones), twigs, and pieces of string. If something disappears, a jar lid, or a safety pin, I sometimes find it in one of Clem's caches. If so, I move it to a new place. He moves it back. I start keeping caches of my own. Behind the baby's dresser, in the corner of an open storage box, behind the laundry hamper. I make piles indoors and outdoors. Clem takes from my piles and I take from his. Objects go back and forth from pile to pile, from place to place.

The object does not seem to matter so much as the "exchange." And Clem is not infallible. He never keeps track of any number bigger than five. He may go several days paying no attention to his caches. But the fact that he keeps track at all amazes us.

50

\*     \*     \*

In the summer evenings we take walks. Holding Tamar against my stomach, with Clem on my shoulder, we go off toward the river. Sometimes Keith carries Clem in his hat—the same hat Clem had been brought home in. He squats in the bowl, extends his neck, rests his head on the brim, and rides along with half-shut eyes.

Darkness slowly envelops familiar landmarks: houses, barns, fenceposts, mailboxes. The bank of the irrigation ditch, overgrown with sumac and tamarisk, becomes a long, low snake-shape disappearing into the distance. The sky glows with the sun's dying light—sometimes a wild, angry fire-red, sometimes a soft, soothing gray-violet. We walk along, Keith and the baby and I, Clem clucking in his throat. A breeze stirs and flutters the hair on top of Tamar's head. Her eyes grow heavy with sleep and close. Birds of dusk flit and dart over our heads: nighthawks, swallows, swifts, virtuoso bug-gatherers of evening and night. We see bats, or think we do. They fly so fast and are so small we have to wonder. But they are there, skimming over the ditchwater, catching vast numbers of insects.

The river: cool and wide. It shimmers and ripples, silvery-surfaced in the last light of day. A gentle, steady current flows in the middle of the stream—countercurrents swirl and gurgle in the

51

reeds along the banks. Pungent mud is an elemental boundary where water and land converge.

We set Clem down at the river's edge. Fading light shines on the mud's moist surface. Placing his feet carefully, Clem begins to walk. Clumps of mud cling to his toes. He lifts a leg, shakes his foot, puts it down, lifts the other leg, shakes that one, puts it down, and so it goes. Sometimes the mud falls off, sometimes it holds fast.

Pecking, jabbing, probing with his beak, he turns up wiggly things—ribbon worms, nematodes, and seed-shrimp, animals that inhabit the mud. There are salamanders and smaller creatures like scuds and water fleas. Clem shows us a world we have never seen before: tiny forms living out one stage of their life cycles in the mud. It is a miniature world: water beetle and mayfly larvae with hairy antennae, segmented worms, nymphs as slender as needles, parrot-jawed crickets, and multitoed millipedes, residents of the river's banks.

Why does he stop just there? We must go back and see.

He has something in his beak—squirming and dripping with mud, it does not look like much. He shakes his head, holding the prize in his beak. It's only a worm, but Clem is pleased.

A large, dark, hairless spider runs across the mud, leaving no trace. Clem jabs at it, misses, drops

his worm, and hops onto a matting of decaying grasses half-floating on the water. Debris drifts by in the slow water closest to shore. Clem shows a brief interest in the current. One foot squishes into the muddy water while the other foot, four toes grasping the matted vegetation, anchors him.

He changes his mind. A quick hop and he's up the bank, coming up behind me. "CAWCAWCAW! CAWCAWCAW! CAWCAWCAW!" Time to pick him up. Keith holds him, trying not to get mud on his shirt. Clem is too muddy to ride home in Keith's hat.

There are no gradual transitions with Clem— he is either full of life, eager for the game, or tired and wanting to be carried. He is either busy with what concerns him, or collapsed in a heap and crying for attention.

What does a raven's tail look like?

It is wedge-shaped and perfect for wagging.

A raven uses its tail for balance and steering, in flight and on the ground. The tailfeathers are called rectrices, or "steering feathers."

Clem wags his tail when visitors come up the drive—wags his tail, bobs his head, and bursts out with: "CAWCAWCAW! CAWCAWCAW! CAW-CAWCAW!"

A visitor may be surprised to find a raven grasping shoelaces, if there are any, and pulling away. If there are no laces, Clem hammers on shoetops with his beak. If there are buckles, he tries to unhook them. Clicking in his throat, beating his wings, he greets all visitors by pecking at their feet.

Those familiar with Clem lift him up and carry him inside on a shoulder or an arm.

Clyde ignores visitors—unless he is afraid of them. If he is afraid he draws himself up into a taller, skinnier shape, his eyes huge and unblinking, and stands rigid until the object of his fear goes away. If his jesses are not hooked up he vanishes to one of his hiding places—and remains there until the coast is clear.

One day a small child comes to visit. She plays

with Clem. They have a tug-o-war with a piece of string and a game of "chase."

Clem loves chase games. He races around like a mad thing: leaping, flapping his wings, dashing in and out of the house, sprinting up the drive, scampering back again, never allowing himself to be "captured." Tiring of this game, Clem allows the little girl to dress him in some of Tamar's baby clothes—a T-shirt and a little gown. His wings are of no use to him in these new clothes, but he walks and hops around the yard garbed in his new raiment, happy to be the center of attention.

When Clem tires of this game he tries to rub the clothes off. Scraping them against a tree trunk does no good. Kicking up dust, trying to reach his dress with his beak, he begins to lose his temper.

In a rage Clem struts (as best he can), kicks, and calls out in a high, shrill voice. Now he is furious at having his wings pinned to his sides. The little girl runs to Clem's rescue—removing the garments as quickly as she can. Clem quiets down. He spreads his wings, ruffles his breast feathers. His agitation drains away. He sits and looks around as if nothing has happened.

The end of July—Clem makes a discovery.

It is a hot day. Shady places offer little relief from the heat. Bees circling, flies buzzing, clouds

55

of gnats over the ditchwater, occasional mosquitoes to slap—we work and rest, rest and work, and do not see Clem wandering off.

A shriek. Shrill, high-pitched, ear-splitting squeals and cackles come from the other side of the ditch—the neighbor's yard. I run, jump over the ditch, tear through the shrubbery, and hear a sound only a pig can make. A pig? (Tamar starts to cry.) The neighbor's pig! What in the world is happening? Where is Clem? (The baby cries louder.) Once through the trees I am met by a whirl of confusion: white chicken feathers, the hens they belong to, the glint of a rooster, his plumage orange-red in the midst of all the white, and what appears to be an unlimited number of very small pigs. Somewhere in the middle of it all is Clem.

Unsuspecting raven has wandered into rooster territory. In a frenzied attempt to keep control of his harem, the rooster races up and down the yard, furious, raving and a little unhinged. A new litter of eleven piglets, left to run free in the daytime, have come to investigate the commotion, and are embroiled in the confusion. It is turmoil: Piglets whining, mother pig trying in vain to collect her young—and Clem, unable to fly away, hunching down on the ground under the melee, trying to make himself small. The rooster will have none of this intruder.

57

Insisting on a confrontation, it spins a devil's dance around the cowering raven while piglets run squealing in all directions. (I no longer hear the baby. Keith must have picked her up.) I walk into the center of the gyrating mass and grab Clem by the nearest end. (It turns out to be his tailfeathers.) I tuck him unceremoniously under my arm, and race back to home territory, leaving the hens, piglets, and sow to sort themselves out.

Work on the house progresses—we finish the hallway between our one big room and the new section. It is nearly August when we finish closing in the new rooms we have been working on. Now comes inside work: laying floors, plastering walls, painting window frames, building a fireplace. We have more room to live in—and Clem has more room to roam around in.

Everything Clem does is noisy and conspicuous. Everything Clyde does is silent and invisible.

Clyde whisks along the floor and along the walls. Wads of dust collect on his feet as he searches for treasures: bugs and spiders, dead moths and crickets—whatever has been left by Clem, who has almost always passed this way before. Covert, surreptitious, Clyde scrounges for provender in all the darkest corners of the house. We feed him, but

58

he likes to supplement his diet with food he finds for himself.

If Clyde has a "best friend," it is Keith. In spirit Clyde is Keith's owl. The two of them are a lot alike: Both like to sit still and look around, as if everything of real importance can only be observed in silence. Keith handles Clyde more frequently than I do—and with better success. The transfer of Owl from perch to floor, from inside to outside perch, is almost always Keith's "job." Clyde stands on Keith's wrist, small and ramrod straight, peering

59

balefully around. Keith strokes his feathers, clucks him under his beak, and whispers to him.

One day Clyde is standing on the floor behind the screen door, looking out. Knock-kneed, reticent little owl. His golden eyes blaze.

Clem approaches from behind. He is clumsy and moves up too fast. Owl spins around, throws himself down into his threat posture, opens his eyes wide and buzzes his war cry. Knees bent, body close to the ground, wings outspread, every feather raised, his neck a fawn-colored ruff we never knew he had: this is Owl at the peak of his wrath.

Clem is warned—but he ignores it.

Owl hisses and chatters. He sounds like electricity, or something sending messages from far away. The sounds seem to come from his knees.

Clem bounds right up to Clyde. This is the first time in three months that Clyde and Clem make physical contact.

In a flash Owl is at Clem's neck, driving sharp talons into his flesh, not wasting a move.

Chattering with fury, swatting his wings, Clyde hangs on despite Clem's dash across the room, around the corner, and down the dark, narrow hallway. Clem makes no sounds. Somewhere along the way, Owl falls off and disappears into the shadows. Clem scurries on, turns the next corner, crosses into another room, and slows down. He

60

looks humbled as he shrugs his wings and realigns his feathers.

Watch as Owl approaches a low-sided bowl for a bath: he steps gracefully, putting first one foot in, then the other, ever alert for a reason to retreat.

Owl likes baths.

Small sprays of water shoot out right and left as he dips his head into the water and swishes it around. He lifts his head and lets water dribble down his front. Squatting low, he flutters his wings, ruffles his feathers, wets himself everywhere: under his wings, under his tail, front side and back. This is a good time to stroke Owl, to rub him under his chin (do owls have chins?), and on the back of his head. Owl grooms himself, turning his head all the way around. It looks odd: Owl facing the wrong way. Each bath is the same. It is one of Owl's few pleasures.

After his bath Owl can't fly. He is skinnier than ever, a mere wisp of dripping feathers with an understructure of bones showing through. The only other time he is as helpless is when he molts. Two or three times a year all of Owl's feathers fall out— or so it seems. For several days, a week at the most, he won't eat. Then it is over. Feathers reappear, his appetite returns.

Twenty minutes after his bath Owl is dry.

Back on his perch he runs his beak through his feathers, nibbles at his feet, and makes soft, chirring sounds.

Clem is getting good at taking leaps. He leaps great distances, and he takes great risks. He leaps onto the table while Owl is bathing—landing right next to Owl's bowl.

Owl goes berserk.

Having given himself over to bathing, Owl is off his guard. But only for an instant.

He flattens himself down in the middle of his bowl, crouching low and weaving a little from side to side. He looks deranged. Disheveled, dripping from his bath, chattering and hissing, he shoots Clem a warning look.

Clem stares back, and then he steps forward to the edge of the bowl, as if to step in. This is too much for Owl. He pounces from bowl to raven's back, seizing hold with his talons. The two birds crash to the floor, feathers flying, water spilling. They roll under the table. Owl is fast. He hooks his beak into Clem's neck and pulls out a few feathers before disappearing into a corner. Clem scrambles to his feet, blinking and shaking. He is reluctant to come out from under the table—as if expecting another attack—but with a little coaxing he finally does.

62

Hours later Owl emerges from his hiding place. His temper is not improved by these episodes of violence with Clem.

While bathing Tamar in the kitchen sink, I put Clem on the counter and let him walk around. One day Clem slips and falls into the water. He throws his head back, flaps his wings and seems frantic. I pick him out of the water, dry him off, and comfort him by holding him close for a minute or two. In ten minutes he is back—looking into the water, bowing low to get as close as he can.

Gripping him firmly with two hands, fingers under his belly, I lower him into the water. First his feet thwack against the water with a splash. Next his tail goes in—wagging up and down (as always); more splashes. He tosses his head back, his eyes wide open and staring. His beak opens, his body stiffens. Then his belly touches water, his head arches backwards even more, his eyes get even wider. I continue to submerge him. His head stays above water, but the rest of him is completely under.

It works. When his feet touch bottom Clem relaxes. He stands there taking it all in. All this time Tamar has been lying on her towel next to the sink, kicking her feet, making fists with her hands, smiling. Clem looks at her—then he looks down. Does he see his own reflection on the surface?

63

Probably not. He lowers his beak and takes a drink. He splashes water over his head. He flaps his wings and wades across the bottom of the sink. He likes it.

After that Clem stands and watches every time I bathe Tamar. He always stays close by, staring intently, and when she is out of the water and dry, he gets in himself.

Clem has favorite water games. If a pan of water is put down in the yard, Clem runs the length of the yard and takes several leaps, the last of which lands him in the middle of the water. Spinning and twirling, he relishes the splash and spatter, the shower of waterdrops that fall on his head. He does this over and over, until the pan pool is emptied by his antics.

To dry off Clem backs up against a warm adobe wall. He spreads his wings, opens his beak, tips his head up toward the sun, and remains still as a statue until he is dry. Owl dries his feathers the same way. As the sun moves, owl and raven follow it, keeping their faces and front feathers to the light.

People want to know how we "house-train" our raven. The answer is, we don't. Clem trains himself. He never leaves droppings when he is in motion. He always stops still to do this, and he leaves his deposits in the same places over and over. He has certain spots he likes best: in the bathroom behind

64

the water heater and in a small space behind the woodpile. The area under his perch in his wire enclosure, where he sleeps each night, has to be cleaned daily. Because Clem has the freedom to come and go, I wonder if his droppings might be accumulating in some secret place I'm unaware of. I envision a pile of white, crusty droppings, inches deep, getting bigger and bigger (higher and higher) as the weeks go by. I never find such a pile. Although Clem spends a lot of time near Tamar, "guarding" her, he never soils any of her blankets, clothes, or the baby basket he perches on. His cleanliness seems innate.

A hot summer afternoon in August. A snake lies in a furrow in the alfalfa field, seeking relief from the heat. A mower is traveling down the field, alfalfa falling away from the cutting edge. The snake almost manages to escape but not quite. Along one side its scaly skin is torn away in gashes that expose the muscle-tissue underneath.

Keith and I find the snake that evening. By now it is hiding in the matted grasses and weeds along the fenceline. From the looks of the snake's wounds we piece together what must have happened.

It is a big snake, perhaps three and a half or four feet long. Normally a snake this size would hiss angrily at us or slither away unseen in the grass.

This snake does not move. We think it is dead, but bright eyes, wide and staring (snakes have no eye-lids), a slight quiver at the tip of the tail tell us it still lives. The injuries are serious, but they may not be fatal.

We decide to try to save the snake by keeping it long enough for its wounds to heal. A foolish decision? Perhaps. Bull snakes are constrictors. Their prey is usually small rodents, but they also eat birds. We don't have to worry about Tamar because, though she is small and helpless, she is much too large for a bull snake. We think of Owl and Clem. Despite obvious risks, Keith and I agree it's worth a try. Keith lifts the snake up, beginning by forcing his hands, palms up, under the heaviest part of the snake's belly. I wrap two hands around the snake's thinner tail end. With his arms slightly extended, his hands firm but gentle on the snake's cold skin, Keith rises to his full height and begins walking home, with me following along. The snake remains still, probably in shock.

Yellow, green, and brown, white belly scales shiny and sleek, this bull snake is a beautiful animal. It is other-worldly and powerful. I touch its body—touch the thick muscles, feel its strength and cool-ness. I study the flawless order of the scales and somehow understand the snake's unconditional wild-ness.

At home we put the snake down on the floor in our big room. It remains motionless. I sit with Tamar tummy-down on my knees. Keith sits next to me. We watch.

Owl is on his platform, jesses hooked. Clem is standing by the front door.

67

Owl looks toward the snake and immediately throws himself into a tumult on his platform, pivoting and reeling in chaotic circles, madly seeking escape but held fast by his jesses. I fear he will break a leg trying to get loose. In the wild Clyde would be an easy meal for such a snake.

Clem, on the other hand, hops toward the snake, turning just in time to avert a collision. At first we are not sure which one to worry about: the snake or the raven. High-stepping, flapping his wings, his beak half-open (and no sound coming

68

out), Clem leaps toward the snake two or three times before Keith grabs him. We have never seen Clem so agitated. Nor Clyde, for that matter. Obviously we cannot all stay in the same room.

Together Keith and I carry the snake into the new section of the house, pushing the hallway door shut and giving the snake the run of the hall and two additional rooms. The first night we both go in two or three times before going to bed—to see what it is doing, to see what it looks like. It lies still when we touch it, unmoving on the stone floor. Getting down on hands and knees I stare at it and see vibrations, shudders, ripples under the snake's belly scales, hinting at life within. I know enough about snakes to know this snake is harmless to man. Despite knowing this I feel afraid. The snake is huge. Its colors against the red brick floor are yellow, brown, and black. The pattern of its scales is perfect. In the dim light of the dying day the snake looks dangerous. It is all my imagination. The snake is not dangerous.

The wounds look terrible, but we do not have a remedy for them. All we can do is leave the snake alone and this we do.

On the other side of the wall the snake is closed off. We believe we have made sure there is no escape. On our side of the wall Owl remains visibly alarmed; there is a look in his eyes we've not seen before. Clem spends a lot of time hopping rapidly up and down, back and forth, along the base of the hallway door. He tosses and jerks his head up and down, from side to side, and cackles deep in his throat. Both birds seem to know the snake is there even though they cannot see it.

On the first day the snake doesn't move at all. We go in and look at it several times. Getting down on my hands and knees, face at floor level, I see muscles pulsing and fluttering. There is an irregular rhythm to the pulses—irregular but persistent. A pale, yellowish liquid oozes from the wounds. It thickens and begins forming a scab over the gashes. There is no odor, and there is no blood. Looking at the snake I see its colors fuse with light from the windows and shadows cast on adobe walls.

On the second day Keith and I go in to look at the snake and see that it has moved. It now lies along the base of the hallway wall, in the darkest part of the hall. The thick curve of its body is almost invisible in the dimness.

For seven days the snake does not eat. We leave small chunks of raw meat along the seam between floor and wall. We know snakes eat fresh prey, but it is something to do, and we need to do something.

Snakes often go long periods without food, but they need water, so we leave water in a pan on the floor. Bull snakes do not see or hear well, but they have heat-sensitive pits in their heads. These detectors pick up the rise in temperature near warm-blooded animals, and tell the snake where its prey is. A rough, heavy nose plate enables bull snakes to travel underground, in burrows, searching out gophers, ground squirrels (and burrowing owls!). For seven days the snake is on my mind—and on Keith's mind, too. Tamar is the only member of the household unaffected by the snake's residence. She goes on as usual: eating, sleeping, smiling, preoccupied with being a baby.

Once, going in to refill the water pan (the water evaporated; I don't think the snake drank any), I decide to search until I find the snake. Sunlight pouring in through a window makes a splash of brilliance on the floor. Nearby, in dark shadow at the base of the wall, the snake lies with its length pressed against the coolness of the adobe. I stand and stare at it. The snake recoils—lifting its body up and around in a spiraling gesture, as if drawing away from my presence. I stand and watch while the snake settles full-length down on the floor again. I am fascinated and mesmerized, cautious and guarded—I want both to watch the snake and leave it alone. A part of the wild world I know nothing about is here in my house. Acutely aware of its restlessness, its distress at being held captive, I feel tension from the snake's body enter into my own.

71

Keith is more inclined to keep away, to avoid the snake unless it is absolutely necessary to go into the part of the house where it is. Keith's quiet, resourceful ways are well known to me. It is usually he who manages best in times of strain or trouble. Something about the snake unsettles Keith, bringing out in him a wariness, and the glint of fear.

It is night and fully dark. Something has awakened me. My skin is cold and clammy and I feel afraid.

Keith is sleeping silently beside me.

I listen to Tamar. The soft, reassuring sounds of her sighs as she sleeps are the only sounds in the room. Clem is on his perch. I can just see the vague shape of his profile in the darkness. And Owl? Where is Owl? Straining to see across the room to where Owl's platform stands against the wall I cannot make him out. It is too dark.

For a long moment I think about getting up to check on Owl, but I sense something close by— something on the bed. I think of the snake—the snake is loose, the snake is here, in the bed. It is the snake that awakened me. How can this be? I think.

Moving nothing but my eyes, I try to find the shape of the snake in the dimness. The snake won't hurt me, and I know this, but I am still afraid. More time passes. It begins to move, and finally I see it. It slides across the covers, undulating sideways across the lower part of the bed. I stay still. I don't know what to do, and I am still afraid. It slides along, weighty and silent, shadowy and close.

I see only the long, thick body in the darkness, no gleaming, shiny scales. Its heaviness on the bed makes my stomach tight. I gently lean against Keith, trying to wake him without startling him too much.

Keith is awake and, unlike me, out of the bed in seconds. He seems to know what is happening before I tell him.

With Keith awake I snap out of my panic. Keith stumbles across the floor to make sure Clyde is all right. He is. Jittery and awake, but unharmed. Tamar and Clem are unaware the snake is loose.

By the yellow-eyed glare of a flashlight we gather up the top sheet of the bed, and the snake with it. The snake stiffens and tries to coil its length around my arms. We are aware of its strength as we struggle to wrap the snake in the sheet (without hurting it) and walk it across the floor to the hallway door.

The hallway door is an unfinished, unplaned door with no lock and latch. Friction keeps it shut. At night we push a chair against it to make double-sure it stays closed. We had forgotten to do this. The snake leaned against the door and its own weight forced it open.

73

\*     \*     \*

The snake's wounds begin to heal. A thin white layer of new tissue grows over the gashes. There are no new scales—just a semitransparent covering of new skin.

As the snake's gashes disappear under their translucent covering, the snake's movement becomes incessant. The snake does not belong with us. I know it. Keith knows it. The owl and the raven know it—and the snake knows it.

It is an enormous relief when we see the wounds are completely healed over and the snake can be let go. It has been awkward to have to keep out of the new part of the house. Ever since the night the snake got loose I sleep less well. I imagine I hear the snake moving about in the next room.

Once the snake is healed and moving constantly, Keith is reluctant to handle it. He is right to be honest about his disquiet, and I am willing to be the one who releases it. I am uneasy about the snake, but I am fascinated, too.

Keith cuts open a burlap sack, making it into a flat piece of material. Together we wrap the snake up in the burlap, turning the extra fabric of the sack around and around the snake's body, like a sheath. We put the snake into the car, allowing it to release itself from its wrapping of burlap once it is securely inside the car. (At this stage Keith is a willing

74

helper.) Again, like the night the snake got loose, it bends and twists in our hands, trying to be free.

With the snake in the car, and all the windows rolled up, I drive off toward the field along the river where we found the snake. During the ride the snake weaves around and around, exploring the inside of the car. Along the floor, up the door on the passenger side, across the back seat, and forward again. It glides along the top of the front seat, inches from my neck. I am utterly shaken by its rhythmic stealth. It takes all the control I possess to keep both hands on the wheel and my foot on the gas pedal.

I get to the field and stop—and open the car door. The snake is on the floor of the back seat, stretched full length and facing me, its head slightly raised. It describes three quick circles in the air with its head before sliding soundlessly out of the car and onto the ground.

Watching the snake slither off into the grass when I let it go is deeply satisfying. For an instant sunlight glints on the snake's healed skin. The white newness of it contrasts sharply with the yellow, brown, and black waves of the snake's design. It is near evening, hot and still. Insects are buzzing, half-awake cows graze in the adjacent field. I hear water murmuring in the irrigation ditch. I squint with my eyes and stare, trying to get one last look at the snake. I sense a mixture of tame and wild, of silence

75

and sound, of dream and reality. I walk back to the car. The air is heavy with heat, and my head is full of imaginings.

There are cats in Clem's life. We do not have cats, but the neighbors do. Our yard often seems an expressway for them—cats sauntering, slinking, picking their feline paths through the bushes. Bold cats, shy cats, belligerent cats, smug cats. When cats destroy the predawn stillness with their howling and yowling, Clem shoots off his perch like a lit firecracker. He races in circles and chases shadows until the sounds die away. He never tries to find the source of the caterwauls. He just runs in circles.

Some cats become Clem's pals. Our neighbor across the road has cats that have litters all the time. Clem and the kittens generally get along—he accepts the fluffy, saucer-eyed meowers tumbling around him. Strutting and displaying his chest feathers, caw-caw-cawing, tossing back his head, he entertains many bands of kittens that venture into our yard.

Once he takes hold of an especially small kitten and drops it into Keith's lap. The kitten does not object to being carried in a raven's beak. Keith receives the kitten and Clem hops off to get another. He transports the second kitten in the same way: gripping the skin at the back of the kitten's head in his beak, the way mother cats carry their kittens in their mouths. The kittens are too young to notice that this time "mother" has two naked brown legs, four scaly toes on each large foot, dark feathers all over, a big black beak, and wings. Clem only stops carrying kittens when all five lie entangled in a burr-shaped mass in Keith's lap. Clem stands and regards his accomplishment for a moment or two. Then he is off to something else.

Thunder clouds in our part of the Southwest are fearsome and wonderful. Often their dark shapes looming overhead make me feel safe rather than threatened. They form out of extravagant white billows that hang against the mountains. Throughout the day we watch the clouds grow heavier. Long, dark and ominous, they blow down into the valley, eclipsing the light of the sun and bringing rain on summer afternoons.

Water cascades off rooftops in brown torrents, races down mud walls, forms miniature arroyos in the yard. Sometimes it thunders so loudly the sky seems to be breaking apart. Lightning flashes and an eerie blue backlights the trees, giving them an imaginary look.

We run inside to stay dry. Baby and baby bed, Owl, if he is out, raven, and whatever tools must not get wet are gathered up in haste.

Inside, holding Tamar, watching her coo and

77

drool, thinking of nothing in particular, I begin to sense something is missing. Keith, Tamar, Owl. Where is Clem?

Surely Clem is bright enough to seek shelter from the rain. Or is he? I peer through a crack in the door. Rain falls in such dense sheets that I cannot see the other side of the yard. Now is not the time to go looking.

Should we go and look anyway? Keith and I discuss it.

Before many minutes have passed, we hear the unmistakable sound of a raven in trouble. Between cracks of thunder and the clamor of rain comes Clem's shrill wail: a cross between a screech and a shriek, loosed to the wind, over and over. Giving Tamar to Keith, I put on my slicker and venture into the wild wetness.

Following Clem's call proves to be difficult. The pandemonium of the storm makes it hard to distinguish his sounds from other sounds. Up one side of the yard, down the other. Is he hidden in the bushes? Out by the road? Nothing. Nothing but rain. Water shoots down the irrigation ditch, tears roots out, pulls plants from their moorings, swishes them away. Wind fills my ears. The bird's call persists, a wailing on the wind.

I walk under every tree in the orchard. No Clem. As I walk back toward the house his cry seems louder. I glance over the fence between our place and the neighbor's, and there he is, sitting mournfully in a wet heap, the rain pounding on him. He apparently simply squatted down where he was when the storm broke—and proceeded to yell.

Looking at him I have to wonder. Is this a bright bird?

Clem trembles as I put him inside my raincoat. Instantly my shirt is dripping. I begin to shake as I absorb the cold from his body.

Inside Keith envelops the soaked bird in a flurry of warm, dry terry cloth. At first he cannot stand up. I decide he has caught something—a terrible cold, pneumonia, or both.

He sits. He stares. He shivers. If birds had teeth, Clem's would have chattered for a long time. After a while he stands up. His feathers dry. The blue membranes around his eyes pull back, and his eyes are bright again. Before long he is cackling away, grumbling and muttering to himself, mimicking the water dripping into the gutter. Raising and lowering his head in quick successive nods, the sound that comes out of his throat is Clem's version of spattering rain.

We build a fire to warm us all.

The rain cools everything off. It washes down

79

the hard crust of dust that layers everything. It softens the light, creating an intimacy between land and sky. The rim of the earth glows with a silvery light, a band of brilliance almost as bright as the heart of the sun. Above and below this band is shadow: the departing rain clouds above, the darkening hills below.

On these cool evenings we sit by the fire. Keith likes to make things—usually toys—out of pieces of wire. He makes tiny bicycles with wheels that really turn, horsemen on spindle-shanked horses, and birds with outstretched wings, using Clem as a model. Sometimes we play chess or just talk. We like watching Tamar as she lies on her back, her hands trying unsuccessfully to capture her feet.

Owl wanders around on the floor, prowling along the edges of the walls. Stiff-legged, he casts an enormous shadow by firelight. When we do not see him we hear him. His toenails make a scratchy sound as he pursues some wondrous thing to eat.

Owl comes and stands directly in front of the fire. We look at him. He looks at the fire. A small bird with dust-colored feathers, some of them sticking out as if bent the wrong way. Knees a little crusty, toes the same.

Looking from Owl to the fire and back again, something tells me I should grab him, but the instant passes and then it is too late.

Owl runs headlong into the pile of burning logs. He is a goner for sure.

But in a split second he darts out again—from the opposite side of the fire. He has entered on the left, found a way around the back of the fire, and come out on the right. He is entirely unhurt, not even singed.

How he did this we never know. Nor why.

I have seen meadow voles become disoriented in terror and race directly into a fire, incinerating themselves. But Owl has seen fires before. And burrowing owls are not voles.

He never tries this trick again. And a good thing, too.

Later that night I put Clyde on his platform and hook up his jesses. I make sure he is fine. Still

dust-colored, still crusty-kneed, still glaring out of half-open eyes, he keeps his miraculous secret.

Ravens are scavengers and eat whatever is available. To Clem, hopping across the road and eating the food that belongs to the neighbor's dog is not stealing. It is doing what comes naturally.

Soulful of eye, pendulous of tail, the neighbor's dog spends most of his time sleeping in the shade of a silver poplar. The dog is a large, shaggy mutt— part sheep dog, maybe a little German shepherd. No one knows. A homeless animal (there are countless of them in New Mexico), he wandered in one day, and the neighbors kept him because he was gentle and kind. They farm their land and have cats, children, a flock of chickens, and some goats. Though the dog is a street urchin, a ragamuffin, he avoids confrontations of any kind.

One day when I cross the road to visit the neighbor and have a cup of tea, Tamar is on one hip, Clem on my shoulder. As we approach, the dog half-rises out of his slumber under the tree. Thinking better of it, he slumps down again—a ruglike shape on the ground. The neighbor and I sit outside and talk. Children are usually the topic of conversation. The neighbor has three small daughters, ages one, four, and six. She reassures me about matters regarding the care and feeding of a baby girl, namely Tamar. Clem hops up on the edge of the dog's dish. Using his beak as a poker he inspects the contents, decides it is acceptable fare, and proceeds to eat it. The dog blinks a few times but lets Clem have the food. Clem scours the bowl clean.

For Clem it is an easy victory, and it gives him a cockier attitude and a much bigger stomach. When he wants some of the dog's food he simply crosses the road and helps himself. The neighbor's dog finds himself in an awkward position. He declines to

chase Clem off, so he must sit and watch, mournfully, as his food disappears.

That Clem is making repeated visits becomes obvious in two ways. First, he comes up the dirt drive like an overstuffed clown, waddling and weaving, belly distended. It is easy to see he has scrounged a large meal somewhere. He smells like dog food (an unmistakable aroma), and bits of it cling to his breast feathers.

Second, the neighbor herself tells me. She has ignored Clem the first few times—thinking he couldn't possibly eat very much. But after several of his visits—with the bowl left clean empty—she resorts to calling me.

Working things out means no food can remain in the dog's dish after he has been fed. It means watching him to make sure *he* eats the food. Clem cannot be trained. Even feeding him more at our house does not help. In the end the dog's bowl is no longer placed outside, and Clem resumes his normal silhouette.

Late summer. We take walks in the afternoons, Tamar, Clem, and I, Tamar usually in her bamboo baby stroller, a rickshawlike contraption with wheels. The stroller is constructed like an armchair, with armrests and a footrest. It has a hood that wobbles from side to side. We go to visit friends—Tamar looking like an Arab princess in her peculiar stroller, pink dress, bare feet. Clem grips the hood with his toes. He jumps from hood to footrest to armrest to hood, clucking and rattling. If someone comes along, Clem positions himself at the foot of the stroller, head up, wings spread. The newcomer cannot greet the baby without meeting Clem first. He is a sentry on her stroller, just as he is a sentry on her sleeping basket.

One of our neighbors has an unusual assortment of animals. Her name is Lucia and she lives a mile or so down the road in an old adobe house built in the Spanish style, with rooms around a central patio. Cottonwoods grow in the patio. An old willow tree grows there, too, its branches drooping low enough in some places to touch the ground.

Lucia has a pond (she calls it a lagoon). The edges of the pond are speckled with the tracks of ducks, geese, and swans. She keeps ducks from all over the world, and she has the biggest, whitest goose I have ever seen.

The goose honks a loud, cacophonous honk the minute it sees visitors approaching. The size of the goose makes it an imposing obstacle, and the noise it makes adds to its effectiveness. When Clem sees the goose for the first time he hangs back—it is the first time I see Clem hesitate.

I know the goose from past experience. Bowing,

with a hand outstretched in greeting, I speak in a low, submissive tone. The goose ignores me and takes aim at Clem.

Charge! It barrels forward with its head near the ground, a powerful, determined guardian in pursuit of an intruder. Clem starts running in erratic circles, flapping and cawing wildly. The goose checks its speed only when I grab Clem around the belly and hold him up in the air over my head.

Tamar sits against her pillows, wide-eyed, her mouth a small, dark hole. I stuff Clem under my shirt and begin to walk calmly back and forth in front of the goose, repeating: "See! No raven! It went away! All gone! No raven!"

Honking loudly and weaving heavily from side to side, the goose finally moves off. We make it to the front door, to the patio—and there, in the safety and seclusion of the inner courtyard, I put Clem down. He blinks a few times and goes off to peck for bugs in the grass. After that I enter Lucia's gate only with Clem securely tucked inside my clothes.

The season turns and we work longer hours, knowing winter to be near. We stack bales of alfalfa from the fields, to be sold as feed during the coming winter. We shuck corn and pick apples. I make apple butter over an outdoor fire, spooning and stirring the hot, sweet-smelling mixture around and around in a big pot. The air smells ripe.

Late September. Harvest time. Clem begins to walk off and require rescue many times a day. It is a nuisance to have to stop everything and follow calls from the wayward raven.

Each time one of us goes to find him he is in a tree, or a bush, or sitting forlornly on the ground, mussed-up and unhappy. His behavior perplexes us: Why is he so jittery and frightened? We decide to sit and watch him for a while.

This is what we see: Clem beats his wings, now full-feathered and strong. They slap and flap vigorously. He dances around on his feet at if on hot ground. Hopping forward, wings up, wings down, hopping faster and faster, each hop taking him farther than the previous hop—each hop less of a landing—until, finally, he leaves the ground completely and is airborne.

These first tries end in a variety of ways.

One way he lands abruptly on his stomach after a very short flight, his wings useless appendages. In another, he gains height and distance only to have it appear he has failed to consider direction. He turns sharply in the air, loses momentum, throws his wings straight up, and plummets to earth like a stone. Sometimes he gets quite high in the air—

higher than the roof of the house—but seems to lose courage. Looking down he forgets to flap his wings. Again he falls to the ground in a heap, his breath knocked away.

We live on flat land, the trees nicely spaced with bushes in between, an ideal place for a young raven to learn to fly. Lots of room for long takeoffs and gentle, gliding landings.

Clem manages to miss all the soft spots, sail right past the best bushes, crash land instead of float down, and end up exhausted, tousled, and screeching. Fortunately his calls carry. I hear him, and, looking all around, I finally see a tiny, black spot creating a commotion in a distant bush or tree.

His landings in trees are especially troublesome to us. If the tree cannot be climbed there is always the ladder. But sometimes the ladder is half a mile away, or more. One time I shimmy up a tree, coax Clem to a lower branch where I can grab him, reach for what I think is a substantial part of him, and end up with a fistful of feathers. Clem lands on the ground, unhurt but furious.

Landings in bushes are simply a matter of untangling raven feathers and limbs from branches and leaves.

After these crashes Clem needs consolation, comfort, and reassurance. We carry him home, speaking gently and petting him.

88

In the wild Clem would have taken to the air sooner. Learning from his parents, he might have flown a month earlier. With us Clem is a late bloomer. With us Clem has it made. He is content to live on the ground for a long while.

Eventually he truly flies. His first successful flight takes him in a wide circle all around our neighborhood, within sight of our house, our yard, of Keith and Tamar and me watching. He learns to do somersaults, rolls, fly upside-down, and land gracefully. His takeoffs remain the least fluid part of his maneuvers. A series of bounding hops, with wings arched up, head stiff, beak a little open, carry him across the ground until (finally) he rises into the air. Takeoffs are especially unwieldy when his belly is full. But after the first success, he always makes it into the air.

We think he might leave us once he knows how to fly.

# Winter

Owl is sick. He won't eat, and the light is gone from his eyes. He stands very still. Feathers fall in dusty heaps all around him—too many feathers. It is not time for Owl to molt.

How do you tell what is wrong with an Owl? Keith holds Clyde in one hand, fingers gently pressing his chest to keep him still. With his other hand he raises Clyde's wings. Lifting up feathers with his fingers, Keith discovers that Owl has dandruff; dandruff and scaly patches of rough red skin.

Owl is too small, too fragile, to go long without

food. We take him to a friend who is a veterinarian and an ornithologist. We take Clem along, too. We shall find out, at last, after ten months, if Clem is male or female.

We learn Clem is male.

We learn Clyde has mites. Patches of scaly skin, loss of appetite and feathers, and dandruff—all from mites. Clyde had mites when he came to live with us. But he was not this sick then, and we were able to cure him—we thought—by dusting him with insecticide. This time it is more serious.

Keith and I wonder if Clyde has had mites all along, if the tiny, almost invisible parasites were present but Owl was strong enough to fight off a serious infestation. Good food, sunlight, baths, and exercise all seem to be what Clyde thrives on. Why he would be ill now we do not know.

Mites are too small to be seen without a magnifying glass. Parasitic arachnids (spider family) that live on other animals and birds, they can be fatal because they draw off energy and resources, finally killing the animal or bird they feed on. Various species of mites are so specialized they live only on bird feathers, under bat wings, in monkey lungs or bee tracheae.

Now we must again dust Clyde with insecticide, but it is risky. Too much of it and Clyde succumbs to the "cure." Too little and the mites have him.

We are told to feed Clyde special food. The food is a concentrated mixture of vitamins, protein, and medication. It comes in capsules that must be "forced" down his throat. Keith assumes full responsibility for this task. Clyde becomes even more of a one-man bird now. Clyde is also stubborn. When Keith comes near to douse him or feed him he throws himself flat down into his threat posture, skinny wings spread, chattering, hissing, and buzzing. Keith holds him under the wings and around his chest, his fingers clasping firmly but gently to keep Clyde immobilized. With his other hand Keith presses the capsule against Clyde's beak until he is "forced" to open his mouth. In one quick move Keith thrusts the capsule down Clyde's throat, pushing with one finger to make sure it goes down and stays down. After this procedure it takes a few minutes for Keith to soothe and reassure the frazzled owl.

It is to make you feel better, Owl!

He does not understand.

For ten days we treat Owl. He has to be kept isolated from everyone else, including Clem. We set up a "private" perch for Owl in the corner of the storage room. For ten days he lives, standing more still than ever, losing more feathers than ever (I never knew he had so many), refusing to eat anything at all. Keith is usually successful in getting the

capsules down, but still Owl grows weaker. Keith begins to worry about the harm it does Clyde to be force-fed. It is a brutal, if necessary, process. We both look in on him many times in a day, always hoping for improvement, never seeing any.

On the morning of the eleventh day we find him lying face down in a pile of feathers, his twiglike legs straight and stiff.

The sadness I feel over Owl's death surprises me. He has crept into my heart, captivated me with his brave yellow eyes, won me with his stoic, humorless ways.

94

Keith feels it even more. Clyde has been "Keith's bird" (Clem is "mine"), and there are few words to express what Keith feels. There is guilt (did we do all we could, or should?); there is sadness; and above all there is the feeling of being wrong about keeping a wild creature captive.

We bury Clyde under the cottonwood tree. We burn his jesses, his platform, all his things. We clean around his perch area, and we worry about Clem getting mites. We take to scrubbing Clem's perch area once a week with a mixture of water and strong soap. We mourn our small, lost friend.

It is difficult to say what Clem does and does not notice about Clyde's disappearance. I sense that he "knows" Owl is gone. Keith and I tell each other a similar fate cannot befall Clem.

One morning we wake to a white light shining in through the windows. Snow has begun to fall in the night, and is still falling soundlessly, encompassing the world, silent, eternal, deep. Little caps of snow crown each fencepost. A white mound stands on every mailbox. Tree limbs are coated and layered. Snowflakes fall as the sun comes up, softening the light. Clouds break into clumps, milky and thick, with a cold blue sky in between.

We get up and make a fire. After breakfast we bundle Tamar in her warmest clothes, put on our

95

coats and hats, and head out into the yard. Clem sits on my shoulder. He hunches down, his head between his wings, as if the cold bothers him. Through the thickness of my coat I feel the grip of his toes as he rides along. Every now and then he leans against my face, his shiny black feathers rubbing against my cheek. We walk up the fenceline toward the river. Neither Clem nor Tamar has seen snow before.

Tamar rides on my hip, holding on with one arm and waving the other in the air, trying to capture snowflakes as they blow by. She has on a red cap. Snow collects on top of her head and scatters when she turns this way and that. The air sparkles. Clem hops down to the snow-covered ground. Up to his belly in white powdery flakes, he hops forward. His feet send up puffs of snow. He spreads his wings and races ahead of us, running up the path along the fence. "CAWCAWCAW! CAWCAWCAW! CAWCAWCAW!" His calls get louder and louder, more and more excited. He lifts himself in flight, turns, and comes down again—landing in a little cloud of white fluff, his landing punctuated by his calls. Soon other birds come. Ravens appear overhead, flying higher than Clem. They circle around and around, their calls ringing down on our ears. Clem flies up and joins them, then lands close by, calling all the while: "CAW-

CAWCAW! CAWCAWCAW! CAWCAWCAW!"

Tamar opens her mouth and tries to taste the instantly dissolving crystals. Licking, reaching with her tongue, she is mystified. Snowflakes come, and are gone, all in the same moment. Waving a mittened hand around her head, she creates a small flurry of snow. She pauses now and then to stare at the snow—as if doing so will tell her what she wants to know.

Clem spends the morning frolicking in the air, racing along the ground, eating snow and tamping it down with his feet. His tracks are everywhere. He stands on the thin, bare branches of the willow along the ditch, shakes them, causing snowflakes to shower down around his head. He waddles up and down on the top wall of the house, using his beak to toss snow right and left. He is not cold. He loves it.

Winter settles in. Dark, gloomy days of dampness and cold alternate with brilliant sunny days and cloudless skies.

Winter means fires in the fireplace, playing chess by the fireside, Keith whittling toys for Tamar—trucks with wheels that don't turn, wooden dolls, blocks she can build with, and toy spoons. Owl used to sit on Keith's knee at times like this. We think of him, and miss him. Sometimes we cook our evening meal over the fire. Tamar, Keith, Clem, and I sit and eat and watch orange flames flicker and cast shadows on adobe walls. Tamar especially loves to watch the shadows. The world outside seems not to exist.

On bright winter days, Tamar plays in the yard. Snow-suited, booted, and mittened, she crawls around in old snow, leaf litter, and debris from the previous summer's construction. Pieces of wood and empty nail boxes become beloved toys. Clem runs in circles around her, springing in and out of reach as she waves her arms around trying to catch him. He flies to a low branch, calls out "RAWK! RAWK! RAWK!," makes Tamar laugh, and flies to the ground again.

Clem still watches over her. I can count on him to sound a warning if someone comes up the drive. He flies off on his own now and then, but never for very long, and never far.

Clem develops habits as he becomes more independent. He likes to fly next door to the neighbor's house and sit on a window ledge. He sits on the ledge and taps on the glass with his beak. A series of taps, always the same number in the same sequence, with pauses in between, usually brings someone to the window to open it. Clem goes inside and "plays" with the neighbor children. When he is ready to return home he goes to the window and

taps on it: the same pattern of taps. Someone opens the window and Clem flies back to us.

This first winter some of Clem's caches are under layers of rotted snow at the bases of trees. To get at them he scratches and scrapes with his feet. He uncovers last summer's treasures and sometimes adds more. He takes buttons and bits of wood. Once I find a small animal bone in one of his caches. He moves things from inside to outside, from outside to inside. He loves being out, no matter how cold it is.

On bright days Tamar and Clem and I tramp up the fenceline path. Clem flies in circles over our heads, or scampers along on the ground, stopping to poke his beak into a ground-beetle burrow, or examine a pile of decaying alfalfa, or kick up old leaves.

On stormy days Clem perches in one of his preferred places, grooms his feathers, sleeps a lot, and eats. When all of us are confined to the house because of a snowstorm or cold rain, Clem seems content to be quiet, to remain inside. He seems to enjoy the chance to draw inward, stay by the fire, and keep warm.

The season turns again. It has been almost a year since Clem arrived. Almost a year since Tamar was born. Tamar is thinking about walking. Clem's feathers begin to fall out. Feathers start piling up under Clem's favorite perches: the top of the tallest bookcase, the highest windowsill, the top of the door leading to the hall. Tamar's first tentative steps coincide with my gathering up handfuls of Clem's discarded feathers, as if to save them. (I do save a few, and make an "Indian" headdress for Tamar.) It is Clem's first molt. His juvenile plumage is falling out and his adult plumage is growing in.

The new feathers are sleek, shiny bluish-black. His tailfeathers are twice as long as before. The wedge shape of his tail is more pronounced. Wing feathers, called remiges, or "rowing" feathers, include large flight feathers (primaries), and smaller feathers (secondaries). The feathers outlining Clem's body, contour feathers, grow in neat, perfect layers. His legs are black. His feet no longer seem too big for his body. A shaggy ruff of feathers around his neck is especially visible when he perches and grooms.

Tamar explores the house on all fours, occasionally standing up to hold on to something and take a few steps before reverting to hands and knees. She, too, collects Clem's feathers. Sitting with a fistful she tickles her cheek. Keith and I decide to have a birthday celebration for Tamar and Clem together.

I make a chocolate cake. On top is written, in

red candy letters: "HAPPY BIRTHDAY TO TA-MAR AND CLEM!" There is chocolate ice cream in the freezer.

We set up the table outside. The neighbors across the road, Lucia, and a few other friends arrive and settle down on the wooden benches around the table. Tamar crawls in and out the doorway, between the yard and the house, and manages to get stepped on several times.

She cries and Keith comforts her. Clem stands on the tabletop in a beam of sunlight, his feathers shining. He takes four giant strides across the table and walks right into the cake. (He must have decided the cake was a solid object.) He seems as amazed as everyone else to find himself up to his knee-joints in this sweet chocolate concoction. Flapping his wings (he has a wingspread of almost four feet now), he pulls himself up out of the mess and flies off to clean himself up.

The cake looks ruined: a jumbled heap on a plate. Together with our guests we eat what we can of it (no one is squeamish) and consider the disaster typical of what happens with a raven in the family.

# Second Summer

Tamar's second summer—and Clem's. Tamar is no longer nursing. I can leave her with a sitter, or with our neighbors across the road, and be gone for long stretches of time—if I choose. Keith and I decide to take a trip down the river in a raft.

Far north of the valley where we live, the river flows through deep, narrow canyons of volcanic rock. In spring, water from melted snow roars and rages through these canyons in a climactic, convulsive flow. Turbulent, rolling waves of brown water explode through the narrowest sections of the river gorge with a dreadful fury. Water levels rise and

submerge the beaches at the river's edge. Swirling
water rips past low-lying cottonwoods, pulls off
limbs, and uproots smaller trees. The water is at its
most destructive in May and early June. By late
June water levels fall dramatically—the snow is gone
and water is drawn off for irrigation along lower
stretches of the river. By late summer the river runs
in smooth, low currents, lapping its banks where
poison ivy grows against black rocks in splashes of
bright green. Sagebrush and cottonwood, sumac
and tamarisk, willow and Apache plume, all grow
in thick patches on the slopes of the canyons. The
river is tame, and we take an inflatable rubber raft
and float downstream.

Clem comes with us. (Tamar stays with the
neighbor across the road.) A box of cookies, a plastic
jug of water are our provisions; suntan lotion and
Clem, our gear. Clem takes to the raft instantly, no
sign of fear or mistrust. He just hops aboard and
stands there as if to say, "All right, I'm here, let's
go!"

Keith, who is over six feet tall, coils himself
into the bow of the raft, a slouch-hat obscuring his
face entirely. I take the stern. We change places
every now and then, taking turns with the small
paddle that is used only intermittently to prod us
away from shore. The river makes a riffling sound—
rhythmic and serene, flowing with a faint pulse.

Along the shore huge horseflies buzz in droopy circles. The heat makes everything seem limp. Dull black rocks, with reddish patches on them, lie in heaps and tumbles on the slopes. The river is half-asleep, like Keith in the bow.

We glide easily along, soothingly, smoothly, turning this way and that as the river's flow demands, generally staying midstream where the strongest currents are.

In a flash Clem is off. Flying up against the walls of the canyon he is at first hard to see: black against black. But Clem is moving and the walls are still. His lifting, swooping form takes shape before our eyes. He dives for something. What can it be?

For several minutes we cannot make out what he has.

And then we see.

Flying toward us, his beak half open, soundless, Clem skims across the water, raises his wings, comes in for a perfect two-point landing. Clutched in his talons is a small, black-and-yellow garter snake about ten inches long. It is very much alive.

Clem has no desire to eat it. The capture is what matters to Clem.

The little snake wiggles and stretches itself in an effort to get loose. Keith jumps to the rescue (of the snake)—grabbing Clem with one hand and the snake with the other. Clem spreads his toes, releasing the snake instantly. In five minutes we have pulled ourselves up on shore. Keith lets the snake go. It wriggles off into the rocks. Clem stands looking surprised (it all happened so fast!), and we are ready to continue downriver.

There are no more astounding events this day. We float, we watch eagles soar over the canyon rim, we eat our cookies, slap at flies. Clem rides along with us, or flies up against the hot, black canyon walls. When we get home in the evening, Tamar is very happy to see us.

Other trips this summer take us to the mountains for backpacking, and to the river again for more rafting. Clem always accompanies us. On hiking trips he sits on top of my pack and rides along half-asleep, bobbing gently up and down in rhythm with my step. Sometimes Tamar comes too, riding along in a baby carrier that resembles a knapsack.

On these trips I carry Tamar and Keith carries most of our gear. Clem's added weight is noticeable—he weighs a little more than two pounds—but he flies half the time and does not seem a burden. He divides his time between flying, riding on my pack (or the baby carrier) or on Keith's pack. When he rides with Keith he sits on the pack and rests his head and beak on the rim of Keith's hat. The heat makes him groggy. When we come to a stream Clem plunges in, sloshing and splashing water over himself, taking drinks, letting cold stream water ripple over his back while he bounces up and down. Sometimes we find him gazing as if hypnotized into pools of still water. His own reflection interests him. On camping trips he perches on top of the tent, the front part of the ridgepole his favorite place. He wakes us in the mornings with his "RAWKRAWK-RAWK RAWKRAWKRAWK" morning cry—a cross between a croak and clearing of the vocal chords.

Heat is a problem for Clem. On river trips he stands on the edge of the raft, stretches out his wings, holds his head back, opens his beak and pants. Every now and then he dips into the river to cool off and returns to his place at the edge of the raft to dry. In the late afternoons he soars up against the canyon walls, finds and flies with other ravens, drops down again to keep track of our progress on the water. There seems to be an invisible cord between us—no matter how far away Clem flies (and he often flies away for hours at a time), we feel our connection to him.

We are high in the mountains on a three-day hiking trip. The country is new to us. Tamar rides on my back in her knapsack carrier. Stuffed under her seat are extra warm clothes. Clem rides on my shoulder, or flies off into the trees, disappearing among the silvery-green spruce branches. Keith carries sleeping bags, food, and cooking gear.

We climb up two thousand feet from where we leave the car—from eight thousand feet to ten. Ahead of us we see steep canyons reaching up out of the valleys like gray, gnarled fingers. All afternoon we watch storm clouds rise and thicken against the highest peaks. The cloud shapes look like fists, or horse heads, or huge Indian drums. As the afternoon wears on the clouds drop lower. Finally it is raining on us.

We decide to camp early. I put Tamar under a tree. Despite the protection offered by Keith's wide-brimmed hat on her head, she gets wetter and wetter while we put the tent up. Clem flies off into the forest. Every now and then we hear his calls over the soft pattering of rain.

When the tent is up, we all three crawl in. It's a small tent. I wonder briefly where Clem is while we change into dry clothes. Now that he is an adult, he makes his own decisions about being with us or not.

Evening closes down. A cold, wet rain settles in for the night. We concentrate on making ourselves as comfortable as possible in our cramped space. After a cold supper there is nothing to do but sleep.

Clem has not returned by nightfall so we pull the tent flap closed and turn in. Where can he be? His venturing off has always until now been a daytime affair. He has always come back by dark.

In the night I wake to find Tamar missing. Our arrangement is that she sleeps with me, in my sleeping bag, while Keith sleeps alone in his. I feel all around in the darkness trying to find her small, lumpy form. No Tamar. Opening the tent flap (the flap is pulled shut, not snapped), I peer intently into the dimness. There in the glow of hazy moonlight I see her. Sitting alone in the vast, voiceless silence, about fifteen yards from the tent, she appears perfectly content. The rain has stopped. The forest is a mute, noiseless place. Stars can be seen through holes in the cloud cover.

Two more times in the night I retrieve Tamar. I whisper to her about the dangers of crawling off. She is not impressed. Her fearlessness pleases me, her persistence dismays me. Toward morning she sleeps deeply and can be roused only with difficulty when breakfast is ready.

Sunlight streams through heavy tree branches, splashing circular patterns on the ground. The sun warms us while we sit by our small fire. Breakfast, and still no Clem. The morning is as blue as cornflowers. The rain has made the forest smell piney and old. Keith and I talk about what it will

be like not to have Clem anymore: preparing ourselves to accept the fact of his being gone. Tamar
nibbles on a biscuit and I cannot seem to get myself
going—to pull down the tent, pack up the gear, set
off up the trail. What if Clem comes back and finds
us gone?

He does come back. Clem's first night away
ends with the familiar "RAWK!RAWK!RAWK!-
RAWK!"—his morning call—issuing out of the
forest thickness like a signal. He flies into our little
clearing, lands by the fire, races once around it, and
jumps into my lap. Wherever he has been, whatever
he has been doing, no harm has come to him. He
seems delighted to be back.

# Second Fall

Autumn comes and it is cold at night. Clem is as busy as ever. He chases cats—now he can fly low over their heads and menace them. He hops along the top wall of the house calling loudly for cats or anyone to hear. He collects treasures for his caches—shards of broken glass from along the road, brightly colored pebbles, and string. He flies high in the sky with other birds: ravens, crows, and jays. He annoys flocks of smaller birds—sparrows and starlings—by flying into their midst and disrupting their flight patterns. He flies off for as long as a day

at a time. Each time I wonder if he will return. He
does, usually by dusk.

Fall days are bright, cold, and clear. The nights
are luminous. A full moon rises over the mountains.
Looking like a slice of marble, its light swims down
out of the sky to define the hills, the arroyos, and
trees and houses.

Trees lose their leaves in great drifts that need
to be raked up. Clem races into the piles, tosses
leaves every which way with his feet and beak, races
off, dashes back again, messes up
my neat stacks, and flies off into the orchard.

Tamar is playing in the front yard. Crawling
and walking, both, she is wearing a knitted blue cap
with pants to match. She toddles off to cover the
distance between herself and Clem. She walks,
crawls, walks again, and by the time she gets to
Clem, he is gone. She sits down. He has flown into
the orchard but is back again in a few minutes. This
time something is in his beak, a piece of apple. Clem
gets a little drunk on the fermenting windfalls in
the orchard. He pecks at them, acts a little stupefied,
and walks a crooked line. Now he drops the half-
rotted apple into Tamar's lap.

He lands next to her, hops around her, cackling,
rattling, and cawing. Tamar claps her hands and
laughs at him. She tries to catch his tailfeathers as
he races past. The two often play together for half

an hour at a time—Clem dropping treasures into her lap from one of his caches or from the fields: stones, bottle caps, bits of wire, small animal bones, and dead bugs. Tamar checks out everything he brings her, sometimes tasting, sometimes not. Whatever it is she examines it closely.

November. A crystalline morning, bare tree limbs sharp against a dazzling sky. A good day to walk in the fields. The orchard is finished for the year, the apples all picked or left to decompose on the ground. Harvesting is over. Alfalfa has been mowed, raked, and baled, and the bales stacked at the ends of the fields or carted off to barns. Our own hay is stacked, ready to be sold. In the cornfields, dry stalks, once green and golden, lie in shreds and tatters on the ground.

The first frost is past, yet flocks of crows still plunder the cornfields, searching for kernels fallen and forgotten in the tangle of leafstalk. Raucous, strident, rasping, and clamoring, the flocks rise and fall in the air. Some settle on fenceposts, telephone wires, or trees. Even as they sit, their discordant calls are noisy in our ears.

A northern harrier flies a few feet off the ground, tilting from side to side, hunting for mice and other small mammals. A slim hawk, with long, narrow wings and a white rump, it shares its hunting

grounds with rough-legged hawks. The rough-legged
hawks hunt exclusively for rodents. They are heavier
birds with black bands on their shorter white tails,
and black at the bends of their wings and on their
bellies. A Mississippi kite dives right before our
eyes as we hike across the fields to the river. It
catches something and takes it to the top of a
telephone pole to eat. The kite flies with swallowlike
grace. It is plain gray on its underside with a notched
black tail. As we walk along we see redtails, the
most common hawk of all. The redtails nest in
cottonwood groves and feed in open country. Their
tails are uniformly reddish on the upper side, a
pinkish color underneath.

Rapacious, predatory hawks—the colors of falling leaves: red, gold, brown, and gray.

Clem flies off with the crows. It is hard to pick him out amidst all the others. A closer look and we see him: He is bigger than the others. His neck ruff is fluffed out, his head is huge, and of all of them he is the most extraordinary flyer. He flies with wonderful ease, clearly enjoying it.

Ravens fly from the mountains to the river, and back again, every day. Like the crows, they, too, come to glean what they can from the wintry fields.

Clem flies off to join the raven flocks the same way he joins flocks of crows. We wonder *when* Clem will fly off and never come back.

People say: "How can you keep a captive bird?"

And we answer: "Clem is not captive. He is free to come, free to go . . ."

For Clem there appears to be no confusion. Resting on my shoulder, or flying in wide circles surrounded by other ravens, Clem is all spirit and energy, and not captive.

Late November. It is hunting season. Along the river people shoot doves, geese, and ducks. Up in the mountains they hunt deer, elk, mountain sheep, and bears.

Early one misty morning we take a walk to the

river. The air is still and heavy. It smells like fog, burning leaves, and ooze. A thin layer of ice coats the mud at the river's edge. As the ice melts, the flowery patterns etched in its surface slowly disappear.

Clem rides on Keith's shoulder for a while, and when we get to the river he flies off into the trees. On this cold, hazy morning we imagine ourselves alone. We are in a place safe from hunters, far enough from the fields they like to hunt in. But suddenly someone close by begins to shoot. We see no one. The shots root us to the ground.

Keith instantly begins to call Clem. In a high, strained voice, he calls out: "CLEM! CLEM! CLEM!"

The shots stop. Keith strides off into the trees, still calling Clem's name.

Minutes pass. I stay where I am among the trees, afraid to go forward, afraid to go back. Tamar rides on my back in a baby carrier. I pull her out of the carrier and clasp her in front of me. We wait.

Silence. Every bird is still. The shots have quieted every living creature in the woods. It seems forever before I see Keith's form walking quickly toward me through the trunks of the cottonwoods.

He holds Clem in two hands, as if with special care. Something is wrong, I know it at once.

Clem's left wing has been grazed. There is a gash just below the "elbow." Clem looks stunned, but not in pain. Someone apparently aimed right at him, or so it appears. I always wonder, afterward, if he felt anything at all—besides the shock of the blow.

Our greatest concern is not Clem's recovery from his wound but whether this will change him, alter his spirit, or dull his enthusiasm. We need not worry. Not only does he recover quickly, his recovery is uneventful. Within a few days, he flies just as wildly, races just as crazily, hops just as happily as he had before.

Snowstorms come and leave drifts of snow against the doors and walls. The sun comes out and melts the snow away. Clem flies high in the winter skies, or ambles along the ground looking into gopher holes. When we walk to the river, Tamar walks the whole way. We go more slowly so she can explore. She likes to be carried home. Clem goes away for a day—or for a day and a night—and every time he does I prepare myself. But he always returns.

Early spring. Clem is full-grown and still curious about the rooster next door! But now his forays into rooster territory are aerial; he avoids direct encounters. Flying low over the willows, he lands on the roof of the chicken house. He sits and glares down at the hens, adjusting his feathers and rattling in his throat. The hens ignore him. The rooster struts about uselessly.

Hens often roost in the trees on warm days— our trees, the neighbor's trees, the trees all around. Clem flies into the trees, jumps from limb to limb, upsets one hen after another, until they drop from the branches like small, feathery bombs. When they hit the ground they run off beating their wings and cackling. The foolish hens eventually make their way back up into the trees, only to be disturbed once more. When the hens drop out of the trees in our yard, Tamar loves to try to catch them. She never can.

Once, in the apple orchard, I see Clem on the ground in the middle of a circle of ravens. Clem is either the raven in charge or the raven being persecuted. The ravens around him make harsh, scolding sounds, as if demanding attention. They dance around him in high, bouncy hops. I imagine Clem has been a rascal and is being rebuked. Or he has summoned all of his friends in order to make a proclamation. In the end I simply watch with no idea what is going on. Eventually the visiting ravens all fly away.

Late spring. Clem's and Tamar's second birthdays have come and gone. A friend telephones to say his dog has dropped a small, wet, gray mass on the back doorstep. Our friend thinks whatever it is must be dead. It has been raining, and it is cold. How can anything survive the bad weather *and* being carried around in a dog's mouth?

Our friend takes the little gray mass of feathers indoors, unfolds it from itself, and discovers it to be a baby screech owl. Cottonwood trees growing thick and close around our friend's house are full of screech owls. The owlet had fallen out of its nest and the dog had found it. It has no wounds, no visible damage, and within an hour it is standing its fullest height (very short), yellow eyes glinting, ear tufts standing straight up.

Screech owls are the smallest of the nocturnal owls. They build year-round nests in almost any environment, from desert to mountains to eastern forests.

Our friend wants to know if we will take the owlet and make a home for it until it can be returned to the wild.

We do. But we do not name it. We want no more tragic owl figures in our lives. We even get a cage for the owlet because we are afraid it might get away into the yard and become cat food.

The cage has a latch on it. The first night the owlet is in the cage Clem unlatches the door, and away the owlet goes. We find it hiding in a corner. The doors and windows are shut, so it can't get

outside. Clem treats the situation like a responsibility: It is his responsibility to release the little owl from the cage. Several tries at fixing up a Clem-proof latch fail. We resort to using a tiny padlock. This Clem cannot undo.

At first the little owl spends most if its time huddled in a corner. After two or three days it perks up. It eats everything we offer it (spiders, flies, dog food, hamburger meat, bits of raw chicken liver), and drinks water from a small dish we put into the cage. At one point it stands in its water and seems to be trying to take a bath. Clem stands at the side of the cage and watches. He works at the wires with his beak, as if trying to bend them. He does not understand the cage at all.

The owlet gets stronger. It starts flying from one end of the cage to the other, without enough room to really get under way. It beats itself against the sides of the cage until it's exhausted. It is time to let it go, since it has a good chance of survival at this stage and is rebelling violently against confinement.

We drive to our friend's house. After talking to him about where the dog might have found the owlet we all walk into the woods in the presumed direction. Owl nestlings sometimes leave the nest before they can fly and are fed by their parents as they scurry around on the ground. They spend a portion of their growing-up time flightless but are also adept at foot travel. Our little owlet is well past the stage of being stuck on the ground. He knows how to fly. This makes his chance for survival fairly good. We think his parents, and nestmates, might still be in the area.

We walk into the woods carrying the cage.

Clem rides on Keith's shoulder, Tamar on my hip.

We open the cage and the owl flies a short distance and lands on the ground. Clem starts to jump down but Keith catches him just in time.

We walk away, looking back again and again, hoping to see the owl fly off. It stays on the ground. We never know its fate.

On the way back, a large flock of ravens settles into the treetops. Big, black, and boisterous, they fill the air with their raspy, throaty sounds. Grooming, chattering, socializing, they bounce from limb to limb, the tree branches giving with their weight.

Clem flies up to join the flock.

We walk on, looking up now and then to see if we recognize Clem among the other ravens. We do. He is one of the biggest, one of the best flyers. When it is time to go home we call him: "CLEM! Clem! Clem!"

No answer. No response. No raven.

The ravens are flying off downriver. We can see them disappearing among the trees. We call some more. We leave and go home.

This time something tells us he is really gone for good. We both feel it.

"CAWCAWCAW! CAWCAWCAW!" It is early in the morning several weeks later. I go outside and look up into the sky. There Clem is, circling around. He lands on the wall. He struts up and down, rattles in his throat, and cocks his head. Even though it is early May the mornings are cold. Clem's feet leave tracks in a thin layer of frost on top of the wall.

I speak to him: "Where in the world have you been? I know—you cannot tell me, but I wish you could . . ."

I pet him. I stroke his throat and ruffle his neck feathers with two fingers. He stands still, hops, stands still again. Then he flies into the sky, circles over the house twice, and is gone.

Clem comes back one more time. He goes to the neighbor's house and taps on the window glass, as he had so often as a young raven. The neighbor comes across the road with Clem on her shoulder. This day he only stays ten or fifteen minutes—and he won't come close to me. Hopping forward, head lowered, he comes near enough for me to reach out and touch him and then he jumps away. He won't let me touch him. He stands still and cocks his head, peering at me out of one eye. Then he is off hopping again, and finally he flies up over the ditch and is gone.

Tamar knows Clem is gone—her friend and playmate no longer brings her treasures from the orchard, or leaves his feathers around for her to gather up and save. She wants another bird, a

replacement. But Clem is irreplaceable. Keith and I agree: no more "captive" wild birds.

One other time I think I see Clem. A flock of ravens flies down into the apple orchard to forage in the tall grass around the trees. One raven sits alone on a tree limb, apart from the others. I stare at it and it stares back. I try to identify it as Clem and cannot. For several long moments we stare at each other. Then the bird flies off with all the other ravens.